On The Fourfold Root
of the Principle
of Sufficient Reason

Ναὶ μὰ τὸν ἀμετέρᾳ ψυχᾷ παραδόντα τετρακτύν,
παγὰν ἀενάου φύσεως ῥιζώμα τ'ἔχουσαν.

("By him who implanted in our mind the quaternary
number, the source and root of eternally flowing
creation."——Pythagorean form of oath.—Tr.)

On The Fourfold Root of the Principle of Sufficient Reason

Arthur Schopenhauer

Translated from the German
by E. F. J. Payne

With an Introduction
by Richard Taylor

Open Court
La Salle, Illinois

OPEN COURT and the above logo are registered in the U. S. Patent and Trademark Office.

© 1974 by Open Court Publishing Company.

First printing 1974
Second printing 1988
Third printing 1990
Fourth printing 1992
Fifth printing 1994

On the Fourfold Root of the Principle of Sufficient Reason
Translated from the German by E. F. J. Payne.

Library of Congress Catalog Card Number: 76-156072
ISBN 0-87548-201-5 (pbk.)

TABLE OF CONTENTS

Contents

Contents

Contents

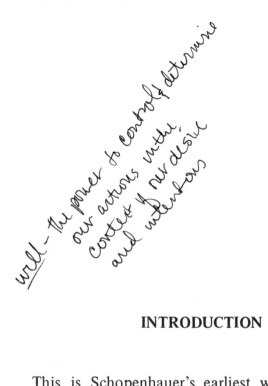
will — the power to control & determine our actions within, context of our desire and intentions

INTRODUCTION

This is Schopenhauer's earliest work, and by many philosophers the most admired, partly because it reflects the philosophical concepts and traditions of his predecessors, particularly in Germany. But by the same token it is the least distinctively Schopenhauerian. The theory of voluntarism, the claim that *will* is the fundamental reality or the very "thing in itself" to which Kant had alluded, hardly appears in this work, though it eventually became the central theme of all Schopenhauer's writings and nourished his deepest and most lasting insights.

By the Principle of Sufficient Reason is meant the dictum that there is a reason, that is, an explanation, for any fact or existent whatever. Schopenhauer formulated it as the claim that "nothing is without a reason for its being," and declared it to be a general formulation of the principle of explanation. We can express this idea otherwise by saying, that everything is intelligible, or that, in the case of anything whatever, whether it be something large or small, great or trivial, there is something *else* in relation to which its existence can be understood and thereby explained.

Schopenhauer clearly considered this abstract principle to be indubitable, knowable a priori, and so nowhere undertakes any defense of it. In fact he thought that there is, strictly speaking, no such thing as *the* Principle of Sufficient Reason, but rather, four quite distinct principles of explanation: These are (i) physical, (ii) logical, (iii) mathematical and (iv) moral. By a *physical* explanation Schopenhauer means the explanation of change in the physical world. By a *logical* explanation he means the explanation or derivation of a truth, a priori. By a *mathematical* explanation he means a geometrical demonstration. And by a *moral* explanation he means, not what one might at first associate with that word, but rather, the explanation of actions, animal or human, in terms of their motives.

It is undoubtedly with respect to the first of these, the principle of explanation involved in physical change, that this work makes its greatest contribution to philosophical thought. Schopenhauer's discussion of the fourth, the principle of explanation as it applies to actions governed by motives, is highly suggestive and original, but was developed in considerably greater detail in his subsequent work, particularly in his *Essay on the Freedom of the Will*. As for the second and third aspects of the principle, that is, its application to logical truth and to mathematics or geometry, Schopenhauer's discussions are rather obscure at crucial points, and have in any case earned their author no great fame.

Schopenhauer's analyses of causation and kindred concepts, which he quite rightly considers to be involved in the Principle of Sufficient Reason as it applies to all change in the physical world, surely rival and probably surpass in their depth and brilliance the more celebrated discussions of David Hume on the same topic. Where Hume grossly oversimplified these problems and left them riddled with paradoxes, Schopenhauer disentangled them and on many crucial points shed light on what had before seemed hopelessly dark. Without attempting a comprehensive summary of his analyses under this first aspect, let us simply note the more fertile of his suggestions concerning the causal relationship, and his claim, which he obviously considered to be of great importance, that perception is the product, not of sensation, but of understanding. This latter claim was not entirely original with Schopenhauer, but there has not been sufficient recognition of its importance even to the present.

Causation.—Causation is the principle of explanation of change in the realm of matter, and Schopenhauer's most important claims with respect to it can be summarized as follows.

(1) Causation is a relationship, not between things, but between changes or states of things. It is therefore misleading and in fact false to speak of things themselves as causes or as effects. It is not, for example, strictly speaking the sun that causes snow to melt, but rather the absorption of the sun's heat by the snow, and this is a change. Similarly, the water that results from melting snow is not caused by the sun or by anything else. Rather, the liquid

state of what was before crystalline is the effect, and such passage from solid to liquid is a change. That which undergoes such change, namely, the water, whether it be in the forms of ice, snow or liquid, endures throughout, and is therefore, as such, neither an effect nor a cause.

(2) The causal relationship between changes is a necessary one, and is not sufficiently described as a mere regular succession. Thus, if one change is in fact the cause of another, then such a change does regularly precede the other, but this by itself does not constitute causation. This, Schopenhauer notes, is indicated by the fact that the knowledge of a causal relation authorizes what he calls a "hypothetical judgment," and what contemporary writers often refer to as "counterfactual inference." Thus, from merely knowing that a given change N is preceded by a change M, we cannot infer that M was the cause of N. Their relationship might be merely one of temporal succession. Further, if we know that a change of kind N is invariably preceded by a change of kind M, then we have a strong basis to infer that all changes of kind M cause changes of kind N; but in asserting this we are asserting more than this regular temporal succession. For we are asserting that, *if* a change of kind M were to occur, then it would be followed by one of kind N. And such a "hypothetical judgment" concerning what has not even occured can hardly be a judgment of temporal succession between actual changes.

(3) The cause of any change is not some one antecedent change, but some one or many changes together with a more or less complex set of conditions in the setting of which those changes take place. Schopenhauer expresses

this idea by saying that an *entire* state is the cause of an ensuing one. If, for example, a window is shattered by the impact against it of a stone, then the cause of its breaking consists not merely of such impact, but of that together with the weakness of the glass, the speed of the stone, the mass of the stone, the angle of impact, and so on. *All* these factors must be taken into account before the change in question is really explained and therefore understood, and hence all belong to the cause, or constitute the "reason" sufficient for the fact in question. The fact that some such factors—the fragility of the glass, for example—are not normally mentioned in such a causal explanation is not because they are thought to be causally irrelevant, but because they are so obvious as to seem to require no mention.

(4) No *thing* ever comes into being or ceases to be. Causes and effects are always changes in what already exists. Hence, the coming into being of a new thing is really nothing but change in what already existed. We think, for example, of a flower coming into being and then perishing, but in fact what has happened in this: Matter, which has always existed, undergoes certain changes, losing certain properties and acquiring others, until at a given point in time and space it has the properties of a flower. Subsequently, these particular properties are replaced by others, and we say that the flower has perished. The entire process can be described completely in terms of changes of state of what already exists, and therefore the principle of causation never requires one to speak of any *thing* as springing into existence.

(5) From this it follows that the metaphysical and theological notions of a "first cause" or a thing ("God") which is the "cause of itself" are absurd. God, if such a being exists, can be no physical cause of anything, nor can the world be an effect, either of God or anything else. Causes and effects are exclusively changes of state *of* or *within* the world. And there can be no such "first" cause, any more than there can be a "last" effect, for it is the casual law that *every* change is preceded by another, and similarly, followed by still another. Causation, Schopenhauer notes, is not like a hired cab which one dismisses once he has arrived at his desired destination.

(6) The causal law is known a priori, and is not derived from experience alone. This follows from the consideration that it applies, Schopenhauer thinks, to every *possible* experience, and hence cannot be derived entirely from actual experience.

(7) Neither laws of nature nor forces of nature are themselves causes. Laws of nature are instead rules, in accordance with which the forces of nature manifest themselves. It is therefore misleading to speak, for example, of gravity or electricity causing something. The gravitational attraction of bodies is in accordance with rules (laws of nature), which are rules of change, and it is always such changes that are causes, strictly speaking.

(8) A body that is in a given state, whether it be one of motion or rest, must remain in that state unless some other change supervenes to alter it. This rule Schopenhauer calls the law of inertia, and it is but a corollary of his analysis of causation. Similarly, that which changes, which is matter or

substance, is eternal. This too follows from Schopenhauer's analysis, and he calls it the law of the permanence of substance.

Perception.—It was common in Schopenhauer's day, as it is in our own, to think that *sense perception* consists simply of sensation, that is, of the stimulation of the organs of sense. These sensations, it is commonly thought, are then interpreted by the mind, and thus used in understanding, reasoning, and intellection generally.

Schopenhauer, on the contrary, argues at great length, and evidently quite conclusively, that perception is *itself* the work of understanding, and cannot possibly result from sensation alone. Sensation is nothing more than a process in the region, as Schopenhauer puts it, of "the skin." Such a process can neither be, nor by itself yield, knowledge of what lies beyond it.

This claim of Schopenhauer's can perhaps be expressed in this way. That there should be certain changes occurring, say, on the palms of one's hands, or on the retina of the eye, is one thing. That a man should perceive, say, that a rope is moving through his hands, or that a tree is visibly in front of him, is something quite different. The first kind of fact, consisting of a mere change in the region of the skin, can in no way be turned into the second kind of fact *except* by an act of understanding. Therefore, the first kind of fact, which is the fact of sensation, cannot be converted to the second which is perception, except by such intellection or understanding. It does therefore follow that perception is not mere sensation. It is sensation supplemented by understanding. When a rope is pulled through a man's hands, there immediately results a change on the surface of his hands and in the nerves. That is a sensation. But the fact of such a physical change in the skin is infinitely far from another fact, that something (a rope) is felt to be moving in a given direction through the hands. The latter is a perception. It is also quite obviously a judgment, or something that can be true or false. And it is therefore, equally obviously, an act of understanding.

This claim of Schopenhauer's seems both incontestable and important—important because, if for no other reason, it has been so little noted by thinkers who have written on perception. Its significance is rather far-reaching. It indicates, for example, the sense in which the objective world, which we naively suppose is merely "given" to sensation, is in fact a creation of the understanding. No such world, Schopenhauer notes, just "walks into our brain" through the senses.

The doctrine of the intellectual character of perception is supported by the most commonplace experiences, the implications of which are so often unnoticed. Thus if one views the landscape lying on his back head down on the side of a steep hill, then his sensations are all reversed, that is, upside down, from what they are normally; yet the landscape does not appear to be upside down. Similarily, if one bends down and views the world through his legs. Now it might be said that, in such cases, everything does in fact look upside down, but that one *reasons* that it really is not, the basis for such a rational inference being one's knowledge of the special conditions of perception. This, however, is not so, for the world still appears right side up, without any reasoning on the matter. An easier example to grasp is

objective world is a creation of understanding

that of simply tilting one's head this way and that. This *because of understood* produces no illusion of the world swinging up and down, like a teeter-totter. The world seems just the same, even though one's sensations quite obviously do not.

From these considerations, and an abundance of others like them, Schopenhauer concludes that understanding is a common possession of both animals and men, since most animals are quite plainly capable of perception. What distinguishes animals from men is men's possession of reason, which is entirely different, and which is involved in perception only in a very indirect way. Thus, understanding can produce illusion, in which case things perceptually *seem* unalterably different from what they *are* but reason, while it can explain the illusion, cannot banish it. The sun and moon, for example, will always *look* like relatively small balls from the earth, no matter how thoroughly reason may instruct us to the contrary. Similarly, a roadway *looks* much farther away to a man twenty feet above it, than to one twenty feet to one side of it, even though both may perfectly well know the actual distance. Reason, accordingly, can distinguish truth from error, but this will by itself not help to distinguish reality from illusion, the latter being within the realm of perception, and hence, of understanding.

The philosophical ideas developed in this early work of Schopenhauer's were never abandoned by him, but simply built upon, in the very rich and profound philosophy that he devoted the rest of his life to creating. Thus when, late in his life, a new edition of *The Fourfold Root* was brought out, its author simply added to it here and there, freely referring to other of his writings that were separated from this one by decades. A reader might therefore easily get the impression that this earliest of Schopenhauer's works was one of his latest. Such consistency and singleness of purpose is not altogether common among philosophers.

RICHARD TAYLOR

UNIVERSITY OF ROCHESTER
February 1971

TRANSLATOR'S INTRODUCTION

In the Preface to the First Edition of his principal work, *The World as Will and Representation*, Schopenhauer requires of his readers, among other things, that they "read the introduction before the book itself, although this is not part of the book, but appeared five years previously (in 1813) under the title *On the Fourfold Root of the Principle of Sufficient Reason: a Philosophical Essay*. Without an acquaintance with this introduction and propaedeutic, it is quite impossible to understand the present work properly, and the subject-matter of that essay is always presupposed here as if it were included in the book. Moreover, if it had not preceded this work by several years, it would not be placed at the front of it as an introduction, but would be incorporated in the first book,[1] since this book lacks what was said in the essay, and exhibits a certain incompleteness because of these omissions, which must always be made good by reference to that essay."

Again, in Volume 2, Chapter 18 of his principal work

Schopenhauer discusses his essay *On the Will in Nature* and says that "we should make a great mistake if we tried to regard the statements of others, with which I have there associated my explanations, as the real and proper material and subject of that work, a work small in volume but important as regards its contents. On the contrary, those statements are merely the occasion from which I have started, and I have there discussed that fundamental truth of my teaching with greater distinctness than anywhere else, and brought it down to the empirical knowledge of nature. This has been done most exhaustively and stringently under the heading 'Physical Astronomy,' so that I cannot hope ever to find a more correct and accurate expression of that core of my philosophy thoroughly and investigate it seriously must first take that chapter into consideration."

Finally, in Volume 2, Chapter 40 of his principal work Schopenhauer says that "I make the demand that whoever wishes to make himself acquainted with my philosophy shall read every line of me. For I am not a prolific writer, a fabricator of compendiums, an earner of fees. . . .I have therefore written. . . so that most of what I have to say is to be found only in one place. Therefore, whoever wants to learn from me and to understand me must not leave unread anything that I have written."

No words could express more powerfully and persuasively the need of these two essays for a thorough grasp of Schopenhauer's philosophical system, and so they will always form an integral part of this. The essay *On the Fourfold Root of the Principle of Sufficient Reason* was first published in 1813 and for it Schopenhauer was made a doctor of philosophy by the University of Jena. A revised and enlarged Second Edition was published in 1847 and in this form it represents one of the clearest and most readable essays ever written on the theory of knowledge. To summarize the main points of this essay the chapter on vision from the essay *On Vision and Colours* (Second Edition 1854) has been added as an Appendix to the present translation.

For some years after its publication in 1819, Schopenhauer's chief work, *The World as Will and Representation*, remained unread and unsold and the philosopher was so mortified by the public's lack of interest in his brain-child, that he maintained a "silence of indignation" which was not broken until he published in 1836 the essay *On the Will in Nature*, a second and revised edition of which appeared in 1854. *On the Fourfold Root of the Principle of Sufficient Reason* throws light on the philosopher's consideration of the world as representation or mental picture (*Vorstellung*), whilst *On the Will in Nature* illuminates what he has to say on the world as will; and so these two essays are complementary respectively to the philosophy of the world as representation and to that of the world as will, the two philosophies forming the basic framework of Schopenhauer's system of thought.

A few remarks on translation may not be inapposite. In § 273 of Volume 2 of *Parerga and Paralipomena* Schopenhauer expresses his aversion to translators, many of whom he stigmatizes as "impertinent" and whom he advises to write books of their own and to leave other men's works alone. On the other hand, in § 242 of the same volume he is of the opinion that almost perfect translations of philosophical works are possible into all languages. It would be presumptuous and impertinent of the translator to claim that his translations were "almost perfect," but the persuasion and even exhortation of friends and the desire to make available to the English-reading public the master-pieces of a world-famous philosopher induced him to undertake the long and arduous task of translation.

It is generally conceded by all who are competent to judge that Schopenhauer was among the foremost masters of German prose and the most eminent writer of German philosophical prose. Thanks to his early acquaintance with French literature, he quickly cultivated a lucid, pithy and trenchant style which admirably conveys the exact meaning of his thoughts. Such distinguishing qualities of authorship have facilitated the translator's task, but problems neverthe-less arise from the difference between the English and the German methods of thought and expression. German authors usually prefer to develop a theme synthetically in a lengthy period consisting of several parts and proceed to elaborate their ideas, often taking up to half a page before they clinch their argument. English authors, on the other hand, follow the analytical course and tend to divide up the thread of their demonstration for their readers, for whom long periods are bewildering and irksome and who rarely have the patience to wade through several lines of print in order to reach the main point of the matter under discussion. This fundamental difference has been borne in mind by the translator who has tried to render into readable English the original German without sacrificing the exact meaning or any of the piquancy, pungency and sparkle of Schopenhauer's words.

All philosophers have their own terminology and Schopenhauer was no exception. Here the problem is to select a word or expression which will convey as precisely as possible the real meaning of the original German. The words *Grund* and *Vernunft* afford a good illustration of the difficulty confronting a translator. These two words are often rendered by "reason," but *Grund* means "ground" or "reason" in the sense of a basis on which a theory or action rests; moreover it occurs in the title of the first essay. On the other hand, *Vernunft* is the reasoning faculty, that power of the mind, peculiar to man alone, which is concerned with forming conclusions, judgments, or inferences. Again, confusion may result from a faulty translation of the words *Vorstellung* and *Idee* both of which are usually rendered by the word "idea." *Vorstellung* is found in the title of Schopenhauer's main work and he uses it to express what he himself describes as an exceedingly complicated physiological process in an animal's brain, the result of which is the consciousness of a *picture* there. The English word "representation" is the nearest equivalent to the German word used in this sense, since the mental picture is a "re-presentation" of the data of the senses. Schopenhauer restricts the use of the word *Idee* to the Platonic sense of a timeless essence or universal, a dynamic and creative archetype of existents. It is best translated by the word "Idea" with a capital letter. The usual German word for "idea" is *Gedanke*, which is quite different from

Vorstellung as used by Schopenhauer.

The German text from which these translations have been made is that of the seven-volume edition of Schopenhauer's works, published by F. A. Brockhaus of Wiesbaden (1946-1950) and edited by Dr. Arthur Hübscher, President of the Schopenhauer-Gesellschaft of Frankfurt am Main. This fine edition represents the fruit of more than a century of textual research and emendation and has long since replaced the old German edition from which earlier English versions of Schopenhauer's works were made. These new translations[2] owe much to the scholarship and abundant annotation to be found in that unique edition.

In conclusion the translator desires to express his deep and abiding indebtedness to his old friend Dr. Arthur Hübscher for the valuable help and advice this eminent scholar has generously given, and to Professor Richard Taylor of the University of Rochester, New York for his energetic interest and encouragement.

E. F. J. PAYNE

CROWBOROUGH, ENGLAND

Footnotes

1. *The World as Will and Representation*, trans. E. F. J. Payne (2 vols.: New York: Dover Publications, Inc., 1966), I, pp. 1-91.

2. The translator wishes to express his appreciation to the editor and the publisher of this definitive German edition for their kind permission to make the present translation into English.

AUTHOR'S PREFACE

This treatise on elementary philosophy first published in 1813 when I gained with it a doctor's degree, afterwards became the basis of my whole system. And so it must not remain out of print as has been the case for four years without my knowing it.

Now to send once more into the world such an early work with all its drawbacks and defects seemed to me unjustifiable. For I am mindful of the fact that the time cannot be very distant when I shall no longer be able to make any corrections. Only with time, however, will the period of my real influence begin and I trust that it will be a long one, for I am firmly convinced of Seneca's promise: "Although envy imposed silence on all who lived with you, those men will come who will judge without ill-will and without favour." [Tr.][1] (*Ep.* 79). I have therefore done what I could to improve the present work of my youth and, considering the shortness and uncertainty of life, I must regard it as particularly fortunate that it was granted to me to correct in my sixtieth year what I had written in my twenty-sixth.

Now in this connexion it was my intention to deal leniently with my younger self and to let him have his say as far as possible, and even speak out. But wherever he asserted anything incorrect or superfluous, or even omitted what was best, I had to interrupt the thread of his argument. This has been the case often enough, and many a reader will gain the impression that he is listening to an old man reading a young man's book which is frequently put down so that the old man may indulge in his own digressions on the subject.

It is easy to see that a work, touched up in this way and after so long an interval, could never acquire that unity and finish to be found only in those works that come out at one cast. Even in the style and method of expression, so unmistakable a difference will manifest itself that the discerning reader is never in doubt whether he is reading the old man or the young. For, of course, there is a great difference between the mild unassuming tone of the young man who is still naive enough seriously to believe that nothing but truth can interest all who are concerned with philosophy, and that they will consequently welcome every advocate of truth, and who confidently states his case,—and the firm but occasionally somewhat harsh voice of the old man who in the end was bound to discover into what noble company of tradesmen and submissive adulators he had fallen, and what their real aims were. Indeed, if the old man sometimes boils with indignation, the fair and sympathetic reader will not censure him for this. Have we not seen by now what happens when men professing to aim at truth have always had in view only the intentions of their chief superiors, and when, on the other hand, the *e quovis ligno Mercurius*[2] is extended even to great philosophers, and accordingly a clumsy charlatan like Hegel is confidently stamped as such? Thus German philosophy stands before us loaded with contempt, ridiculed by other nations, expelled from all honest science,—like a prostitute who for shameful remuneration sold herself yesterday to one man, today to another. The minds of the present generation of scholars are disorganized by Hegelian nonsense; incapable of thinking, coarse and stupefied, they become the prey to the shallow materialism that has crept out of the basilisk's egg. Good luck to them! I return to my subject.

The reader will, therefore, have to be content with the disparity of tone, for in this work I could not give separately the later additions, as was done in my chief work. Moreover, it is not important for the reader to know what I wrote in my twenty-sixth and in my sixtieth years. On the contrary, the only important matter is that those wishing to obtain a correct bearing, a firm footing, and a clear insight as regards the basic conceptions of all philosophizing, have in these few pages a little work from which they can learn something sound, solid, and true; and I hope that this will be the case. From the arrangement now given to some parts, we even have a compendious theory of the whole faculty of knowledge. By simply following the principle of sufficient reason, this theory presents the matter from a new and characteristic angle. But it is then supplemented by the first book of the *World as Will and Representation* together with the relevant chapters in the second volume of that work, and by the Criticism of the Kantian Philosophy to be found at the end of the first volume.

FRANKFURT AM MAIN
September 1847

Footnotes

1. *Etiamsi omnibus tecum viventibus silentium livor indixerit; venient qui sine offensa, sine gratia judicent.*
2. "From any piece of wood a god can be carved." [Tr.]

CHAPTER I

INTRODUCTION

§ 1. The Method

The divine Plato and marvellous Kant unite their firm and impressive voices in recommending a rule for the method of all philosophizing, indeed of all knowledge in general.[1] We should comply with two laws, they say, namely with those of *homogeneity* and *specification*; they should be equally observed, neither to the detriment of the other. The law of *homogeneity* tells us to start with kinds by observing the similarities and agreements in things, and also to unite these kinds into species, and these again into genera until we ultimately arrive at the highest concept that embraces everything. As this law is transcendental and essential to our faculty of reason, it presupposes that nature is in harmony with it, an assumption that is expressed by the old rule: *entia praeter necessitatem non esse multiplicanda.*[2] On the other hand, the law of *specification* is expressed thus by Kant: *entium varietates non temere esse minuendas.*[3] Thus it requires that we clearly distinguish from one another the species united under one compre-

1

hensive generic concept, and again the higher and lower kinds included under these species. It requests us to guard against making any jump, and indeed against subsuming directly under the generic concept the lower kinds, or even individuals. For every concept is still capable of subdivision into lower ones, and not even one concept comes down to mere intuitive perception. Kant teaches that both laws are transcendental fundamental principles of our faculty of reason (*Vernunft*) which postulate a priori a conformity of things with them. And in his own way Plato appears to express the same thing by saying that these rules to which all science owes its origin were hurled down to us from the seat of the gods simultaneously with the fire of Prometheus.

§ 2. Its Application in the Present Case

In spite of so strong a recommendation, I find that the second of these two laws has been too little applied to a fundamental principle of all knowledge, namely the *principle of sufficient reason* (*Grund*). Thus although this principle had frequently been stated in a general way long ago, no one had troubled to draw a proper distinction between its extremely different applications, in each of which it acquires another meaning, and which therefore indicate its origin from different powers of the mind. But a comparison of the Kantian philosophy with all previous systems shows us that precisely in the observation of our mental powers the application of the principle of homogeneity with the neglect of the opposite principle resulted in many persistent errors, whereas the application of the law of specification led to the greatest and most important advances. Therefore I may be permitted to quote a passage in which Kant recommends the application of the law of specification to the sources of our knowledge since it justifies my present attempt.

> It is of the highest importance to isolate different kinds of knowledge which in species and origin differ from others and to see that they are not mixed up with those others with which, for practical purposes, they are usually associated. What is done by the chemist in the analysis of substances and by the mathematician in pure mathematics is far more incumbent on the philosopher so that he can define with certainty the part played by a special kind of knowledge in the promiscuous use of the understanding, and can also define the peculiar value and influence of that knowledge. (*Critique of Pure Reason*, Doctrine of Method, Third Section.)

§ 3. Advantage of This Inquiry

Were I to succeed in showing that the principle forming the subject of this inquiry does not issue directly from *one* kind of fundamental knowledge but primarily from *different* kinds in our mind, it will then follow from this that the necessity which it entails as a firmly established a priori principle is also not *one* and everywhere the *same*, but a necessity just as manifold as are the sources of the principle itself. But then everyone basing a conclusion on the principle will be obliged to define exactly which of the different necessities underlying this principle supports him and to give such a necessity a special name (as I am about to suggest). I hope that in this way some advance will be made towards greater lucidity and precision in philosophizing. I regard the greatest possible comprehensibility, to be attained by an accurate definition of every expression, as the absolutely necessary prerequisite for philosophy. We need this in order to guard against error and intentional deception, and to make every piece of knowledge gained in the realm of philosophy a possession more secure which will not be again wrested from us by the later discovery of any misunderstanding or ambiguity. In general the real philosopher will always look for clearness and distinctness; he will invariably try to resemble not a turbid, impetuous torrent, but rather a Swiss lake which by its calm combines great depth with great clearness, the depth revealing itself precisely through the clearness. Vauvenargues has said: *La clarté est la bonne foi des philosophes.*[4] On the other hand, the sham philosopher will certainly not try to conceal his ideas through words according to Talleyrand's maxim, but will rather attempt to hide his lack of ideas; he will shift onto the reader's conscience the incomprehensibility of his own *philosophemes* which arises from a want of clearness in his own thinking. This explains why in some works, in those of Schelling, for example, the didactic tone so often passes into one of rebuke; in fact readers are frequently taken to task in advance for their inability to understand.

§ 4. Importance of the Principle of Sufficient Reason

Its importance is exceedingly great, for it can be called the basis of all science. Thus *science* signifies a *system* of notions, in other words, a totality of connected, as opposed to a mere aggregate of disconnected, notions. But what else except the principle of sufficient reason unites the links of a system? The very thing distinguishing every science from the mere aggregate is the fact that its notions follow from one another as from their ground or reason. Therefore Plato says: "For even true opinions are not of much value until someone ties them together by reasoning from a cause." [Tr.]⁵ is wrong — [Tr.] [5] (*Meno*, p. 385 *Bip.*) Moreover, almost all sciences contain notions of causes from which the effects may be determined, and likewise other notions of necessities of consequents from grounds or reasons, as will be found in our further observations; this has been expressed by Aristotle in the following words: "All knowledge which is of a theoretical nature, or is in any way connected with the theoretical, is concerned with grounds and principles." [Tr.] [6] (*Metaphysics*, V. 1.) Now as it is the assumption, always made a priori by us, that everything has a reason or ground which justifies us in everywhere asking why, this why may be called the mother of all sciences.

§ 5. The Principle Itself

Later on we are to show that the principle of sufficient reason is a common expression of several kinds of knowledge given a priori. Meanwhile it must be laid down in some formula. I choose Wolff's as the most general: *nihil est sine ratione cur potius sit quam non sit.*[7] Nothing is without a ground or reason why it is.

Footnotes

1. Plato, *Philebus*, pp. 219-23; *Politicus*, pp. 62, 63; *Phaedrus*, pp. 361-63, ed. *Bip*. Kant, *Critique of Pure Reason*, Appendix to the Transcendental Dialectic.

2. "The number of entities must not be increased unnecessarily." [Tr.]

3. "The varieties of entities must not be diminished unnecessarily." [Tr.]

4. "Lucidity is the good faith of philosophers." [Tr.]

5. Καὶ γὰρ αἱ δόξαι αἱ ἀληθεῖς οὐ πολλοῦ ἄξιαί εἰσιν, ἕως ἄν τίς αὐτὰς δήσῃ αἰτίας λογισμῷ (*etiam opiniones verae non multi pretii sunt, donec quis illas ratiocinatione a causis ducta liget*).

6. Πᾶσα ἐπιστήμη διανοητική, ἤ καὶ μετέχουσά τι διάνοιας, περὶ αἰτίας καὶ ἀρχὰς ἐστι (*omnis intellectualis scientia sive aliquo modo intellectu participans, circa causas et principia est*).

7. "Nothing is without a ground or reason why it is rather than is not." [Tr.]

CHAPTER II

SUMMARY OF THE MAIN POINTS PREVIOUSLY TAUGHT ABOUT THE PRINCIPLE OF SUFFICIENT REASON

§ 6. First Statement of the Principle and Distinction of Two of its Meanings

The more or less accurately defined abstract expression for so fundamental a principle of all knowledge must have been found at a very early date. And so it might be difficult, and moreover of no great interest, to indicate where such an expression first occurs. Plato and Aristotle do not formally state it as a leading fundamental principle, yet they frequently express it as a certain and positive truth. Thus with a naivety which, compared with the critical investigations of modern times, appears like the state of innocence compared with that of a knowledge of good and evil. Plato says: "It is necessary for everything that happens to happen through a cause; for how could it happen without this?" [Tr.] [1] (*Philebus*, p. 240 *Bip*); and again in the *Timaeus* (p. 302): "All that happens must neccessarily happen by virtue of a cause; for it is impossible for anything to come into existence without a cause." [Tr.] [2] At the end of his book *De Fato* Plutarch cites the following among the chief propositions of the Stoics: "The most important and fundamental principle should be that nothing ensues without cause, but everything occurs according to preceding causes." [Tr.] [3]

In the *Posterior Analytics*, I, 2 Aristotle to some extent states the principle of sufficient reason when he says: "We think we understand everything perfectly when we think we know the cause whereby the thing exists, namely that it is the cause of that thing, and that this could not possibly be otherwise." [Tr.] [4] He also gives in the *Metaphysics Lib.*, IV, c. 1 a classification of the different kinds of reasons or grounds, or rather of principles, ἀρχαί, and assumes eight of these; but this classification is neither thorough nor sufficiently precise. Yet he is quite right in saying: "All principles have in common the fact that they are the first thing through which anything exists, occurs, or is known." [Tr.] [5] In the following chapter he distinguishes several kinds of causes, although somewhat superficially and indistinctly. However, four kinds of reasons or grounds are better stated in his *Posterior Analytics*, II, 11: "There are four kinds of causes: the first consists in what constitutes the essence of the thing; the second in what must necessarily be assumed (as substratum) if a thing exists; the third in what first put a thing in motion; the fourth in the purpose for which it is." [Tr.] [6] Now this is the origin of the classification of the *causae*, generally assumed by the Schoolmen, into *causae materiales, formales, efficientes et finales*, as can be seen from Suárez's *Disputationes metaphysicae, Disp.* 12, *Sect.* 2 et 3, this true compendium of Scholasticism. But even Hobbes (*De Corpore*, Pt. II, c. 10, § 7) still quotes and explains this classification. It is found again in Aristotle's works, and somewhat more detailed and distinct in the *Metaphysics*, I, 3. It is also briefly mentioned in the book *De somno et vigilia*, c. 2. Yet as regards the highly important distinction between a ground or reason of knowledge and a cause, Aristotle to a certain extent reveals some idea of it insofar as he shows at great length in the *Posterior Analytics*, I, 13 that knowing and demonstrating *that* a thing exists is very different from knowing and proving *why* it exists. What he represents as the latter is knowledge of the cause, and what he represents as the former is the ground or reason of knowledge. But yet he is not clearly aware of the difference, otherwise he would have adhered to it and observed it in the remainder of his writings. This, however, is by no means the case; for even where he attempts, as in the passages quoted above, to distinguish between the different kinds of reasons or grounds, the really essential difference, alluded to in the chapter here considered, never again occurs to him. Moreover, he uses the word αἴτιον in general for every ground or reason of whatever kind it may be. Very often he calls even the ground of knowledge, in fact the premisses of a conclusion, αἰτίας, as for example in the *Metaphysics*, IV, 18; *Rhetoric*, II, 21; *De Plantis*, I, p. 816 (Berlin edition), but especially in the *Posterior Analytics*, I, 2, where the premisses of a conclusion are simply called "the causes of the conclusion." [Tr.]⁷ But when two closely related concepts are expressed by the same word, this is an indication that their difference is not recognized or at any rate grasped; for an accidental homonymy of widely different things is quite another matter. But this error is most conspicuous in his description of the sophism "reasoning from what is not cause as if it were cause" [Tr.] [8] in the book *De sophisticis elenchis*, c. 5. By αἴτιον he understands here absolutely nothing but the argument, the premises, and thus a ground or reason of knowledge, since the sophism consists in our proving quite correctly the impossibility of something. But the sophism has absolutely no bearing on the proposition in dispute which we nevertheless profess to have upset by means of it. Therefore it is not here a question of physical causes. Yet the use of the word αἴτιον has had so much weight with modern logicians that they merely stick to it in their accounts of the *falliciae extra dictionem* [9] and explain the *fallacia non causae ut causa* [10] generally as the statement of a physical cause, which it is not. For instance, Reimarus, G. E. Schulze, and Fries do this, and so do all those whom I have come across; only in Twesten's *Logic* do I find this sophism correctly explained. In all other scientific works and dissertations a charge of a *fallacia non causae ut causa* [10] as a rule denotes the interpolation of a false cause.

Sextus Empiricus also gives us a striking example of the way in which the ancients generally were in the habit of confusing the logical law of the ground of knowledge with the transcendental natural law of cause and effect. Thus in the ninth book of *Adversus Mathematicos*, and hence in the *Adversus Physicos*, § 204, he undertakes to prove the law of causality and says: "Anyone asserting that there is no cause (αἰτία) either has no cause (αἰτία) for asserting this, or he has. In the first case his assertion is no truer than its converse; in the second he establishes by his very assertion the fact that there are causes."

We see, then, that the ancients had not yet reached a clear distinction between requiring a reason of knowledge in support of a judgement and requiring a cause for the occurrence of an actual event. Now as regards the Schoolmen of later times, the law of causality was for them just an axiom beyond all investigation. Thus Suárez (*Disputationes* 12, Sect. 1) says: "We do not inquire whether there is a cause of anything, since nothing in itself is more certain." [Tr.] [11] Here they stuck to the above-quoted Aristotelian classification of causes; on the other hand, as far as I know, they were not made aware of the necessary distinction that we are discussing.

§ 7. Descartes

For in this respect we find even our eminent Descartes, the instigator of subjective reflection and thus the father of modern philosophy, still involved in error and confusion that are difficult to explain. In a moment we shall see to what serious and deplorable consequences these have led us in metaphysics. In the *Responsio ad secundas objectiones in meditationes de prima philosophia, axioma I,* he says: "Nothing exists of which it could not be asked from what cause it exists. For this can be asked even in respect of God, not as if he required any cause in order to exist, but because the very immensity of his nature is the *cause or reason* by virtue of which he needs no cause in order to exist." [Tr.] [12] He ought to have said: The immensity of God is a reason or ground of knowledge from which it follows that God needs no cause. However, he confuses the two, and we see that he is not clearly aware of the great difference between cause and ground of knowledge. But with him it is really his intention that mars his insight. For here, where the law of causality demands a *cause*, he inserts instead a *ground of knowledge* because such a ground does not, like a cause, at once lead to something further; and so by this very axiom he paves the way to the *ontological proof* of the existence of God. He became the inventor of this after Anselm had in a general way given merely an introduction to it. For immediately after the axioms, of which the one just mentioned is the first, this ontological proof is now stated formally and quite seriously; in fact it is really expressed already in that axiom, or at any rate lies therein just as readily as does the chick within the egg that has been sat on for a long time. Thus whereas everything else requires a cause for its existence, the *immensitas* implied in the very notion of God who is brought on to the ladder of the cosmological proof, suffices for him in lieu of a cause; or as the proof itself expresses it: "Existence is necessarily contained in the concept of the supremely perfect being." [Tr.] [13] This, then, is the conjuring trick for the sake of which the confusion, already familiar to Aristotle, of the two chief meanings of the principle of sufficient reason was used directly *in majorem Dei gloriam.* [14]

When considered generally and impartially, this famous

ontological proof is really a most delightful farce. On some occasion or other someone ponders over a concept which he has composed from all kinds of predicates. In this connexion, however, he takes care that the predicate of reality of existence is one of these, either plain and unadorned or more respectably wrapped up in another predicate, such as *perfectio*, *immensitas*, or something of the kind. Now it is well known that from a given concept we can extract all its essential predicates, in other words, the predicates without which it cannot be thought, and likewise also the essential predicates of these predicates, by means of purely analytical judgements. Accordingly, these have *logical* truth, in other words, they have their reason or ground of knowledge in the given concept. Therefore the predicate reality or existence is also extracted from that arbitrarily thought-out concept, and thus an object corresponding to the concept is now supposed to exist in reality and independently of the concept!

> Were not the thought so confoundedly smart,
> One might be tempted to call it absurd.[15]

Moreover, the simplest answer to such an ontological demonstration is the following: "All depends on whence you have your concept; if it is drawn from experience, well and good, for its object exists and needs no further proof; on the other hand, if it is hatched out of your own *sinciput*, then all its predicates are of no avail; it is just a phantom of your brain." But in order to gain a footing in the territory of philosophy, wholly foreign to it, where it would very much like to be, theology has had to resort to proofs of this

15

kind, and this stirs up a very unfavourable prejudice against its pretensions. But oh for the prophetic wisdom of Aristotle! He had never heard anything of the ontological proof; but as though he saw into the night of the coming dark ages, detected in them that scholastic dodge, and wanted to bar the way thereto, he carefully demonstrated in the seventh chapter of the second book of the *Posterior Analytics* that the definition of a thing and the proof of its existence are two different and eternally separate matters. For through the one we learn *what* is meant, but through the other *that* such a thing exists. Like an oracle of the future he expresses the sentence: "*To be* does not belong to the essence of a thing, for existence is not an attribute or characteristic." [Tr.] [16] This states that "existence can never belong to the essence of the thing." On the other hand, we can see how much Herr v. Schelling venerates the ontological proof in a long note on page 152 of the first volume of his *Philosophische Schriften* of 1809. Yet we can see something even more instructive, namely, how an impudent assumption of fine airs and swagger are sufficient to throw dust into German eyes. But so thoroughly contemptible a creature as Hegel, whose whole pseudo-philosophy was really a monstrous amplification of the ontological proof, tried to defend this proof against Kant's *Critique*. This is an alliance of which the ontological proof itself might be ashamed, however little in other respects it may be given to blushing. I must not be required to speak with deference about men who have brought philosophy into contempt.

Existence is necessary for anything to exist, therefore, God, a supreme being exists.

[16]

§ 8. Spinoza

Although Spinoza's philosophy consists mainly in the negation of the twofold dualism set up by his teacher Descartes, namely that between God and world and between soul and body, he nevertheless remained wholly true to Descartes in the above-mentioned confusion and mixing of the relation between ground of knowledge and consequent with that between cause and effect. In fact, where possible, he tried to draw from this even greater advantages for his metaphysics than Descartes had drawn for his, for the above-mentioned confusion became the basis of his whole pantheism.

Thus in a concept all its essential predicates are contained *implicite*, and so can be developed *explicite* therefrom through merely analytical judgements; the sum-total of these is its definition. This, then, is different from the concept itself not in content but only in form, since it consists of judgements which are all thought along with it and hence have their ground or reason of knowledge in it, insofar as they show its essence. Accordingly, these can be regarded as the consequences of that concept, such concept being their reason or ground. Now this relation between a concept and the analytical judgements based thereon and capable of development therefrom, is precisely the relation between Spinoza's so-called God and the world, or more correctly between the one and only substance and its numberless accidents. "God or the substance consisting of an infinite number of attributes (necessarily exists)."

[Tr.]^{17} (*Ethics,* I, pr. 11.) It is therefore the relation between the *ground of knowledge* and its consequence; whereas *real* theism (Spinoza's is merely nominal) assumes the relation between *cause* and effect. In this relation the ground or reason remains different and separate from the consequence not merely as regards the method of consideration as in the other relation, but essentially and really and thus in itself and always. For the word God, honestly used, expresses such a cause of the world with the addition of personality. On the other hand, an impersonal God is a *contradictio in adjecto.*^{18} Now in trying to retain the word God to express substance even in the relation stated by him, and in expressly calling such a substance the *cause* of the world, Spinoza could succeed only by completely confusing those two relations, and so by mixing the principle of the ground of knowledge with that of causality. To prove this I call to mind from innumerable passages, merely the following. "It is to be noted that for each thing that exists, there necessarily is a definite *cause* with reference to which it exists. And it is to be noted that this cause, with reference to which a thing exists, must either be included in the existing thing's own nature and *definition* (since it is inherent in its very nature to exist), or be given *outside* itself." [Tr.]^{19} (*Ethics*, Pt. I, *prop.* 8, *schol.* 2.) In the latter case he means an efficient cause, as appears from what follows; whereas in the former he means a mere reason or ground of knowledge. However, he identifies the two and thus paves the way for his intention to identify God with the world. To confuse a reason of knowledge, lying within a given concept, with a cause acting from without, and to put the two on the same footing, is always his artifice, which he has learnt from Descartes. As illustrations of this confusion, I quote the following passages. "All that can come under the concept of the infinite intellect must follow from the necessity of the divine nature." [Tr.] [20] (*Ethics*, Pt. I, *prop.* 16.) But at the same time he calls God everywhere the cause of the world. "All that exists gives expression to the power of God which is the *cause* of all things. (*Ibid., prop.* 36.)–Proof: God is for all things the immanent, not the transcendent, *cause*. (*Ibid., prop.* 18.)–God is the *efficient cause* not only for the existence, but also for the essence of things. (*Ibid., prop.* 25.)–Proof: From any given *idea* some *effect* must follow of necessity. (*Ibid.*, Pt. III, *prop.* 1.)–No thing can be destroyed except through an external cause. (*Ibid., prop.* 4.)–Proof: the *definition* of a thing affirms, but does not deny, its essence; in other words, it asserts and does not deny the essence of the thing. Therefore, if we look at the thing itself and not at external causes, we cannot see in it anything that would be capable of destroying it." [Tr.] [21] This means that, since a concept cannot contain anything that contradicts its definition, i.e., the sum-total of its predicates, so too a thing cannot contain anything that could become the cause of its destruction. This view, however, is brought to a climax in the somewhat lengthy demonstration of the eleventh proposition. Here the cause that could destroy and put an end to a being is confused with a contradiction which its definition contained and which would therefore abolish this. The necessity of confusing cause and reason of knowledge here becomes so urgent that Spinoza can never say *causa* or *ratio* alone, but is always compelled to say *ratio seu causa*; and so this is done eight times on one page in order to cover up the fraud. Descartes had already done the same thing in the above-mentioned axiom.

Thus Spinoza's pantheism is actually only the *realization* of Descartes' ontological proof. In the first place he adopts the above-mentioned ontotheological proposition of Descartes: "It is the very immensity of the nature of God that is the *cause (causa) or reason (ratio)* by virtue of which he needs no cause in order to exist." [Tr.] [22] He says (in the beginning) always *substantia* instead of *Deus*, and now ends by saying: "The essence of substance necessarily involves its existence; consequently substance must be *its own cause*." [Tr.] [23] (*Ethics*, Pt. I, *prop.* 7.) Hence by the same argument with which Descartes had proved the existence of God, Spinoza demonstrates the absolutely necessary existence of the world, which therefore needs no God. This he does even more clearly in the second scholium up to the eighth proposition: "Now as it forms part of the nature of substance to exist, its definition must involve existence as something necessary, and consequently its existence must be inferred from its mere definition." [Tr.] [24] But as we know, this substance is the world. The demonstration to *prop.* 24 says in the same sense: "That whose nature, considered by itself alone, involves existence, is *cause of itself*." [Tr.] [25]

Thus what Descartes had stated only in an *ideal*, only in a *subjective* sense, in other words, only for us, only for the purpose of *knowledge*, namely for proving the existence of God, was taken by Spinoza in a *real* and *objective* sense, as the actual relation of God to the world. With Descartes the existence of God lies in the *concept* of God, and thus becomes the argument for his actual being; with Spinoza God himself is in the world. Accordingly, what was mere reason of knowledge with Descartes is made into reason of fact by Spinoza. If in his ontological proof Descartes had taught that God's *existentia* follows from his *essentia*, Spinoza makes of this the *causa sui*, and boldly opens his ethics with: "By cause of itself I understand that whose essence (concept) involves existence"; [Tr.]^{26}—deaf to Aristotle who exclaims to him: "Existence does not belong to the essence of a thing." [Tr.]^{27} Now here we have the most palpable confusion of reason of knowledge with cause. And if Neo-Spinozists (Schellingites, Hegelians, and others), with whom words are usually regarded as ideas, often indulge in pompous and solemn admiration of this *causa sui*, then I for my part see in *causa sui* only a *contradictio in adjecto,*^{28} a before that is an after, a bold and peremptory order to cut off the endless causal chain. In fact I regard it as analogous to that Austrian who, unable to reach high enough in order to fasten the clasp on his tightly strapped shako, got up on a chair. The proper emblem for *causa sui* is Baron Münchhausen on horseback and sinking into the water, gripping his horse with his thighs and lifting himself and the animal up by means of his own pigtail, with the words *causa sui* underneath.

To conclude, let us glance at the sixteenth proposition of the first book of the *Ethics*, where it is concluded from the proposition, "From the given definition of anything the intellect infers further qualities and properties which in fact necessarily follow from the selfsame definition," that "from the necessity of the divine nature (that is to say, taken as real) infinite definitions and modifications must result in an infinite number of modes." [Tr.][29] This God then undoubtedly has to the world the relation of a concept to its definition. Nevertheless the corollary: "that God is the *efficient cause* for all things" [Tr.][30] is directly connected with it. The confusion of reason of knowledge with cause cannot be carried farther, nor could it have more important consequences than it has here. But this indicates the importance of the theme of the present essay.

The errors of those two great minds of the past arose from a want of clear thinking, and in our own times a small epilogue to them has been provided by Herr v. Schelling since he has endeavoured to add even a third step to the present climax. Thus Descartes had met the demand of the inexorable law of causality that drove his God to extremities, by substituting a reason or ground of knowledge for the required cause in order to set the matter at rest. From this reason of knowledge Spinoza had made an actual cause, and hence *causa sui*, whereby for him God became the world. And now Schelling (in his essay on human freedom) made the reason and consequent separate in God himself; hence he consolidated the thing much more by raising it to a real and substantial hypostasis of the reason and its consequent. For he made us acquainted with something "that is in God not God himself, but his reason or ground, as a primary reason, or rather *groundlessness*." "In truth this surpasses everything." [Tr.][31] Today it is well known that Schelling took the whole fable from Jacob Boehme's *Gründlicher Bericht vom irdischen und himmlischen Mysterio*. But no one seems to know from what source Jacob Boehme himself took the thing, and what is the real birthplace of this groundlessness. I therefore propose to mention it. It is the βυθός, i.e., *abyssus, vorago*, hence the bottomless pit, the *groundlessness* of the Valentinians (a heretical sect of the second century), which impregnated the silence consubstantial with it, and this silence now gave birth to the understanding and the world, as is recorded by Irenaeus (*Against the Heresies*, Bk. I, c. 1), in the following words: "For they assert that in the invisible and unnameable sublimity there pre-exists a certain perfect Aeon, but they call this the primary beginning, the original father, and *abyss.*—But since he is incomprehensible and invisible, and has existed from eternity and without origin, he has lived in great peace and tranquillity during endless aeons of time. They say that, simultaneously with him, insight has existed, and they call this also Grace and Silence. Then that *abyss* once had the idea of letting the beginning of the world emerge from himself, and, just like dropping the seed into the womb, he lowered into the coexisting silence this emergence (to bring forth which had been his idea). But this silence received the seed and became pregnant, and then gave birth to the intellect which was like and equal to its creator and was alone capable of comprehending the greatness of the father. But they call this intellect the only-begotten and the origin of the universe." [Tr.][32] This must have come in some way to the ears of Jacob Boehme from the history of heresy, and Herr v. Schelling accepted it from him in good faith.

§ 9. Leibniz

Leibniz was the first to make a formal statement of the principle of sufficient reason as a main principle of all knowledge and science. He proclaims it very pompously in many passages of his works, giving himself airs as though he had been the first to invent it. But he cannot say any more about it than that everything must have a sufficient ground or reason why it is so and not otherwise; and of course the world must have known this before he did. It is true that he occasionally alludes to the distinction between its two principal meanings, yet he has not expressly emphasized this or clearly discussed it anywhere else. The main passage is in his *Principia Philosophiae*, § 32, and is a little better in the French version of this work entitled *Monadologie:* "In virtue of the principle of sufficient reason, we assume that no fact can be true or real and no judgement correct without there being a sufficient reason or ground why it is thus and not otherwise." [Tr.][33] Compare this with *Théodicée*, § 44, and the fifth letter to Clarke, § 125.[33A]

§ 10. Wolff

Wolff is therefore the first expressly to separate the two main meanings of our principle and to expound the difference between them. Yet he does not establish the principle of sufficient reason in logic, as is done at the present time, but in ontology. It is true that in § 71 he urges the necessity of not confusing the principle of sufficient reason of knowledge with that of cause and effect, but yet here he does not clearly define the difference. In fact he himself is guilty of confusions, since in that very chapter, *De ratione sufficiente*, §§ 70, 74, 75, 77, he quotes examples of cause and effect and of motive and action as proof of the *principium rationis sufficientis*. If he wanted to make that distinction, those examples should have been quoted in the chapter *De causis* of the same work. Now in this chapter he again quotes very similar examples, and once more puts forward the *principium cognoscendi* (§ 876). As this has been discussed already, it is here naturally out of place, yet it serves to introduce the clear and definite distinction between this principle and the law of causality, which then follows, §§ 881-884. Here he also says: "That is called principle which contains within itself the ground or reason for something else"; [Tr.][34] and distinguishes three kinds, namely: (1) *PRINCIPIUM FIENDI* (*causa*), which he defines as "The principle of reason of becoming: The reason for the actuality of another thing; e.g., if the stone becomes hot, fire or the sun's rays are the reasons why heat is inherent in the stone." [Tr.][35] (2) *PRINCIPIUM ESSENDI*, which he defines as "The principle of reason of being: The reason for the possibility of another thing; in the same example the reason for the stone's capacity to absorb heat is to be found in the essential nature of the stone, that is, in the manner of its composition." [Tr.][36] This latter concept seems to me inadmissible. As Kant has shown often enough, possibility in general is agreement with the conditions of all experience which are known to us a priori. From them we know, with reference to Wolff's example of the stone, that changes are possible as effects of causes; in other words, we know that one state can succeed another, if the latter contains the conditions for the former. Here we find as effect the stone's state of being hot, and as cause the preceding state of the stone's ultimate capacity for heat and of its contact with free heat. Now Wolff calls the first-mentioned property of this state *principium essendi*, and the second property *principium fiendi*; but this rests on a delusion arising from the fact that, so far as the stone is concerned, the conditions are more enduring and can therefore wait longer for the others. Thus the stone is as it is and is so chemically constituted that it brings with it a particular degree of specific heat, consequently a capacity for heat which is in inverse proportion to its specific heat. On the other hand, it comes in contact with free heat. All this is the consequence of a chain of previous causes all of which are *principia fiendi*. But it is the coincidence of circumstances on both sides which primarily constitutes that condition, and on this condition as cause depends the heating as effect. Here there is no room for Wolff's *principium essendi*, which I therefore do not admit. I have dealt with this at some length here partly because I shall use the name later on in an entirely different sense, and partly because the discussion helps to make more comprehensible the true meaning of the law of causality. (3) As I have said, Wolff distinguishes a *principium cognoscendi*, and also under *causa* mentions an "impulsive cause or reason determining the will." [Tr.] [37]

§ 11. Philosophers Between Wolff and Kant

In his *Metaphysica,* §§ 20-24 and §§ 306-313 Baumgarten repeats Wolff's distinctions.

In the *Vernunftlehre,* § 81 Reimarus distinguishes (1) *inner ground or reason (Grund)*, his explanation of which agrees with Wolff's *ratio essendi*, while it could apply to the *ratio cognoscendi*, if he did not transfer to things what applies only to concepts; and (2) *outer ground or reason*, i.e., *causa*. § 120 *et seq.* he correctly defines the *ratio cognoscendi* as a condition of the statement; but yet in an example § 125 he confuses it with cause.

In the *New Organon* Lambert no longer mentions Wolff's distinctions, but shows in an example that he distinguishes between reason of knowledge and cause, namely in Vol. I, § 572, where he says that God is the *principium essendi* of truths, and that truths are the *principia cognoscendi* of God.

In his *Aphorismen*, § 868 Platner says: "What is called reason and consequent within our mental representation (*principium cognoscendi, ratio–rationatum*), is in reality cause and effect (*causa efficiens–effectus*). Every cause is a reason or ground of knowledge, every effect is a consequent of knowledge." He therefore thinks that cause and effect

27

are what correspond in reality to the concepts of reason (*Grund*) and consequent in our thoughts; that the former are related to the latter in much the same way as substance and accident are to subject and predicate, or as the object's quality is to our sensation thereof, and so on. I do not consider it necessary to refute this opinion, for everyone will readily see that the relation between reason and consequent in judgements is somthing entirely different from a knowledge of effect and cause, although in individual cases even knowledge of a cause, as such, can be the reason or ground of a judgement that states the effect. (Cf. § 36.)

§ 12. Hume

No one before this serious thinker had ever doubted what follows. First, and before all things in heaven and on earth, is the principle of sufficient reason, namely as the law of causality. For it is a *veritas aeterna*,[38] in other words, in and by itself it is superior to gods and fate. Everything else, on the other hand, the understanding for example, which thinks this principle of reason or ground, and equally the whole world, and also whatever may be the cause of this world, such as atoms, motion, a creator, and so on,—all this exists only in accordance with, and by virtue of, this principle. Hume was the first to whom it occurred to ask whence this law of causality derived its authority and to demand its credentials. His result is well known, namely that causality is nothing but the empirically perceived *chronological sequence* of things and states, a sequence to which we have become accustomed. Everyone at once feels the fallacy of this result; moreover it is not difficult to refute it. But the merit lay in the question itself; this became the impulse and starting-point for Kant's profound investigations, and thus led to an incomparably deeper and more thorough view of idealism than the one which had existed hitherto, and was principally the Berkeleian. It led to transcendental idealism from which the conviction arises that the world is just as dependent on us, as a whole, as we are on it in particular. For by pointing out the transcendental principles as such through which we are able to determine a priori, in other words, *prior* to all experience, something about objects and their possibility, he proved that, independently of our knowledge, these things cannot exist just as they present themselves to us. The resemblance between such a world and the dream is plain.

§ 13. Kant and His School

Kant's chief passage on the principle of sufficient reason is found in a small work, *Über eine Entdeckung, nach der alle Kritik der reinen Vernunft entbehrlich gemacht werden soll*, in fact in the first section under A. Here Kant insists on the distinction between the logical (formal) principle of knowledge "every proposition must have its ground or reason," and the transcendental (material) principle "every thing must have its ground or reason," for he carries on a controversy with Eberhard who had tried to identify the two. Later on in a special paragraph I shall criticize Kant's proof of the a priori, and thus transcendental, nature of the law of causality after I have furnished the only correct proof.

Following these precedents many treatises on logic produced by the Kantian school, for example those of Hofbauer, Maass, Jakob, Kiesewetter, and others, define fairly accurately the difference between reason or ground of knowledge and cause. Kiesewetter in particular states the difference quite satisfactorily in his *Logik* (Vol. I, p. 16) thus: "Logical ground or reason (reason of knowledge) is not to be confused with the general ground or reason (cause). The principle of sufficient reason belongs to logic, the principle of causality belongs to metaphysics (p.60). The former is the fundamental principle of thought, the latter that of experience. Cause concerns actual things, logical reason or ground concerns only representations."

Kant's opponents insist even more emphatically on this distinction. In his *Logik*, § 19, Note 1 and § 63, G. E. Schulze complains of the confusion between the principle of sufficient reason and that of causality. Salomon Maimon complains in his *Logik*, pp. 20, 21 that much has been said about the sufficient reason or ground without any explanation of what is understood by it. On page xxiv of the preface he censures Kant for deriving the principle of causality from the logical form of hypothetical judgements.

F. H. Jacobi says in his *Briefe über die Lehre des*

Spinoza (enclosure 7, p. 414), that there has resulted from the confusion between the concept of ground or reason and that of cause a delusion which has become the source of a number of false speculations. In his own way he also states the difference between them. But, as is usual with him, we find here a good deal more self-complacent phrase-juggling than serious philosophizing.

Finally from his *Aphorismen zur Einleitung in die Naturphilosophie*, § 184, we can see how Herr v. Schelling distinguishes between ground or reason and cause. These aphorisms open the first part of the first volume of Marcus and Schelling's *Jahrbücher der Medizin*. Here we are told that gravity is the *reason*, and light the *cause* of things. I quote this merely as a curiosity, for in other respects such frivolous and reckless talk is not fit to be numbered among the opinions of serious and honest inquirers.

§ 14. On the Proofs of the Principle

We have still to mention that several fruitless attempts have been made to prove in general the principle of sufficient reason, for the most part without defining exactly in which sense it was taken. For instance, Wolff's proof in his *Ontologie*, § 70, which is repeated by Baumgarten in his *Metaphysik*, § 20. It would be superfluous to repeat and refute it here, for it obviously rests on a verbal quibble. Platner in the *Aphorismen*, § 828, and

Jakob in his *Logik und Metaphysik* (p. 38, 1794 edition) have tried other proofs, but in them the circle is readily recognized. As I have said, I shall later discuss Kant's proof. As I hope to show through this essay the different laws of our cognitive faculty, of which the principle of sufficient reason is the common expression, it will follow as a matter of course that the principle in general cannot be proved. On the contrary, Aristotle's remark applies to all those proofs (with the exception of the Kantian which is directed not to the validity but to the a priori nature of the law of causality), namely where he says: "They seek a reason for that which has no reason; for the principle of demonstration is not demonstration." [Tr.]^{39} (*Metaphysics,* III, 6, which may be compared with *Posterior Analytics,* I, 3.) For every proof is a reduction of something doubtful to something acknowledged and established, and if we continue to demand a proof of this something, whatever it may be, we shall ultimately arrive at certain propositions which express the forms and laws and thus the conditions of all thinking and knowing. Consequently, all thinking and knowing consist of the application of these; so that certainty is nothing but an agreement with those conditions, forms, and laws, and therefore their own certainty cannot again become evident from other propositions. In the fifth chapter we shall discuss the nature of the truth of such propositions.

Moreover, to seek a proof for the principle of sufficient reason in particular is especially absurd and is evidence of a want of reflection. Thus every proof is the demonstration of the ground or reason for an expressed judgement which precisely in this way obtains the predicate *true*. The principle of sufficient reason is just the expression of this necessity of a reason or ground for every judgement. Now whoever requires a proof for this principle, i.e., the demonstration of a ground or reason, already assumes thereby that it is true; in fact he bases his demand on this very assumption. He therefore finds himself involved in that circle of demanding a proof for the right to demand a proof.

1. Ἀναγκαῖον, πάντα τὰ γιγνόμενα διά τινα αἰτίαν γίγνε-σθαι· πῶς γὰρ ἂν χωρὶς τούτων γίγνοιτο; (necesse est quae-cunque fiunt, per aliquam causam fieri: quomodo enim absque ea fierent?)

2. Πᾶν δὲ τὸ γιγνόμενον ὑπ' αἰτίου τινὸς ἐξ ἀνάγκης γίγνε-σθαι· παντὶ γὰρ ἀδύνατον χωρὶς αἰτίου γένεσιν σχεῖν (quidquid gignitur, ex aliqua causa necessario gignitur: sine causa enim oriri quidquam, impossibile est).

3. Μάλιστα μὲν καὶ πρῶτον εἶναι δόξειε, τὸ μηδὲν ἀναι-τίως γίγνεσθαι, ἀλλὰ κατὰ προηγουμένας αἰτίας (maxime id primum esse videbitur, nihil fieri sine causa, sed omnia causis antegressis).

4. Ἐπίστασθαι δὲ οἰόμεθα ἕκαστον ἁπλῶς, ὅταν τὴν †αἰ-τίαν οἰόμεθα γινώσκειν, δι' ἥν τὸ πρᾶγμά ἐστιν, ὅτι ἐκείνου αἰτία ἐστιν, καὶ μὴ ἐνδέχεσθαι τοῦτο ἄλλως εἶναι. (Scire autem putamus unamquamque rem simpliciter, quum pu-tamus causam cognoscere, propter quam res est, ejusque rei causam esse, nec posse eam aliter se habere.)

5. Πασῶν μὲν οὖν κοινὸν τῶν ἀρχῶν, τὸ πρῶτον εἶναι, ὅθεν ἤ ἐστιν, ἤ γίνεται, ἤ γιγνώσκεται. (Omnibus igitur principiis commune est, esse primum, unde aut est, aut fit, aut cognoscitur.)

6. Αἰτίαι δὲ τέσσαρες· μία μὲν τό τι ἦν εἶναι· μία δὲ τὸ τινῶν ὄντων, ἀνάγκη τοῦτο εἶναι· ἑτέρα δέ, ἤ τι πρῶτον ἐκίνησε· τετάρτη δέ, τὸ τίνος ἕνεκα. (Causae autem quatuor sunt: una quae explicat quid res sit; altera, quam, si quaedam sint, necesse est esse; tertia, quae quid primum movit; quarta id, cujus gratia.)

7. Αἰτίαι τοῦ συμ εράσματος.

8. *Non causae ut causa*, παρὰ τὸ μὴ αἴτιον ὡς αἴτιον.

9. "Fallacies attributable not merely to words." [Tr.]

10. "Fallacy based on a cause that is not a cause." [Tr.]

11. *Non inquirimus an causa sit, quia nihil est per se notius.*

12. *Nulla res existit, de qua non possit quaeri, quaenam sit causa, cur existat. Hoc enim de ipso Deo quaeri potest, non quod indigeat ulla causa ut existat, sed quia ipsä ejus*

naturae immensitas est CAUSA SIVE RATIO, propter quam nulla causa indiget ad existendum.

13. *In conceptu entis summe perfecti existentia necessaria continetur.*

14. "To the greater glory of God." [Tr.]

15. Schiller, *Wallenstein, Piccolomini*, II, 7. [Tr.]

16. Τὸ δ'εἶναι οὐκ οὐσία οὐδενί· οὐ γὰρ γένος τὸ ὄν: *ESSE autem nullius rei essentia est, quandoquidem ens non est genus.*

17. *Deus, sive substantia constans infinitis attributis. Ethics,* I, pr. 11. *Deus, sive omnia Dei attributa.*

18. "A logical inconsistency between a noun and its modifying adjective" [such as "a round square," "wooden iron," "cold fire," "hot snow." Tr.]

19. *Notandum, dari necessario uniuscujusque rei existentis certam aliquam CAUSAM, propter quam existit. Et notandum, hanc causam, propter quam aliqua res existit, vel debere contineri in ipsa natura et DEFINITIONE rei existentis (nimirum quod ad ipsius naturam pertinet existere), vel debere EXTRA ipsam dari.*

20. *Ex necessitate divinae naturae omnia, quae sub intellectum infinitum cadere possunt, sequi debent.*

21. *Quidquid existit Dei potentiam, quae omnium rerum CAUSA est, exprimit. Demonstr.—Deus est omnium rerum CAUSA immanens, non vero transiens.—Deus non tantum est CAUSA EFFICIENS rerum existentiae, sed etiam essentiae.—Demonstr. Ex data quacunque IDEA aliquis EFFECTUS necessario sequi debet. Nulla res nisi a causa externa potest destrui.—Demonstr. DEFINITIO cujuscunque rei, ipsius essentiam* (essence, quality, as distinct from *existentia,* existence) *affirmat, sed non negat; sive rei essentiam ponit, sed non tollit. Dum itaque ad rem ipsam tantum, non autem ad causas externas attendimus, nihil in eadem poterimus invenire, quod ipsam destruere.*

22. *Ipsa naturae Dei immensitas est CAUSA SIVE RATIO, propter quam nulla causa indiget ad existendum.*

23. *Substantiae essentia necessario involvit existentiam, ergo erit substantia CAUSA SUI.*

24. *Quoniam ad naturam substantiae pertinet existere, debet ejus definitio necessariam existentiam involvere, et consequenter ex sola ejus definitione debet ipsius existentia concludi.*
25. *Id, cujus natura in se considerata* (i.e., definition) *involvit existentiam, est CAUSA SUI.*
26. *Per causam sui intelligo id, cujus essentia* (concept) *involvit existentiam.*
27. Τὸ δ εἶναι οὐκ οὐσία οὐδενί.
28. "A logical inconsistency between a noun and its modifying adjective" [such as a "round square," "wooden iron," "cold fire," "hot snow." Tr.]
29. *Ex data cujuscunque rei definitione plures proprietates intellectus concludit, quae revera ex eadem necessario sequuntur,* that *ex necessitate divinae naturae* (that is to say, taken as real) *infinita infinitis modis sequi debent.*
30. *Deum omnium rerum esse CAUSAM EFFICIENTEM.*
31. *Hoc quidem vere palmarium est.*
32. Λέγουσι γάρ τινα εἶναι ἐν ἀοράτοις καὶ ἀκατονομάστοις ὑψώμασι τέλειον Αἰῶνα προόντα· τοῦτον δὲ καὶ προαρχήν, καὶ προπάτορα, καὶ βυθὸν καλοῦσιν. . . . Ὑπάρχοντα δὲ αὐτὸν ἀχώρητον καὶ ἀόρατον, ἀΐδιόν τε καὶ ἀγέννητον, ἐν ἡσυχίᾳ καὶ ἠρεμίᾳ πολλῇ γεγονέναι ἐν ἀπείροις αἰῶσι χρόνων. Συνυπάρχειν δὲ αὐτῷ καὶ Ἔννοιαν, ἣν δὲ καὶ Χάριν, καὶ Σιγὴν ὀνομάζουσι· καὶ ἐννοηθῆναι ποτε ἀφ᾽ ἑαυτοῦ προβαλέσθαι τὸν βυθὸν τοῦτον ἀρχὴν τῶν πάντων, καὶ καθάπερ σπέρμα τὴν προβολὴν ταύτην (ἣν προβαλέσθαι ἐνενοήθη) καθέσθαι, ὡς ἐν μήτρᾳ, τῇ συνυπαρχούσι ἑαυτῷ Σιγῇ. Ταύτην δὲ, ὑποδεξαμένην τὸ σπέρμα τοῦτο, καὶ ἐγκύμονα γενομένην, ἀποκυῆσαι Νοῦν, ὅμοιόν τε καὶ ἴσον τῷ προβαλόντι, καὶ μόνον χωροῦντα τὸ μέγεθος τοῦ Πατρός. Τὸν δὲ νοῦν τοῦτον καὶ μονογενῆ καλοῦσι, καὶ ἀρχὴν τῶν πάντων. (*Dicunt enim esse quendam in sublimitatibus illis, quae nec oculis cerni, nec nominari possunt, perfectum Aeonem praeexistentem, quem et proarchen, et propatorem, et BYTHUM vocant. Eum autem, quum incomprehensibilis et invisibilis, sempiternus idem et ingenitus esset, infinitis temporum seculis in summa quiete ac tranquillitate fuisse.*

36

Unâ etiam cum eo Cogitationem exstitisse, quam et Gratiam et Silentium (Sigen) nuncupant. Hunc porro BYTHUM in animum aliquando induxisse, rerum omnium initium proferre, atque hanc, quam in animum induxerat, productionem, in Sigen (silentium) quae unâ cum eo erat, non secus atque in vulvam demisisse. Hanc vero, suscepto hoc semine, praegnantem effectam peperisse Intellectum, parenti suo parem et aequalem, atque ita comparatum, ut solus paternae magnitudinis capax esset. Atque hunc Intellectum et Monogenem et Patrem et principium omnium rerum appellant.)

33. *En vertu du principe de la raison suffisante nous considérons qu'aucun fait ne sauroit se trouver vrai ou existant, aucune énonciation véritable, sans qu'il y ait une raison suffisante, pourquoi il en soit ainsi et non pas autrement.*

33[A]. For a discussion by the late Mr. Francis J. Payne concerning the incorrectness of Schopenhauer's statement see *Jahrbuch*, **33** (1949-1950) of the Schopenhauer-Gesellschaft, 133. [Tr.]

34. *Principium dicitur id, quod in se continet rationem alterius.*

35. *Ratio actualitatis alterius; e.g., si lapis calescit, ignis aut radii solares sunt rationes, cur calor lapidi insit.*

36. *Ratio possibilitatis alterius: in eodem exemplo, ratio possibilitatis, cur lapis calorem recipere possit, est in essentia seu modo compositionis lapidis.*

37. *Causa impulsiva, sive ratio voluntatem determinans.*

38. "Eternal truth." [Tr.]

39. Λόγον ζητοῦσι ὧν οὔκ ἐστι λόγος ἀποδειξεως γὰρ ἀρχὴ οὐκ ἀπόδειξίς ἐστι. *(Rationem eorum quaerunt, quorum non est ratio: demonstrationis enim principium non est demonstratio.)*

CHAPTER III

INADEQUACY OF PREVIOUS STATEMENTS AND THE OUTLINE FOR A NEW ONE

§ 15. Cases That Are Not Included Under the Previously Established Meanings of the Principle

From the summary given in the previous chapter, it follows as a general result that a distinction was drawn between two applications of the principle of sufficient reason, although this was done only gradually and very tardily, and not without frequent lapses into error and confusion. The one application was to judgements which, to be true, must always have a ground or reason; the other was to changes in real objects which must always have a cause. We see that in both cases the principle of sufficient reason authorizes us to ask *why*, a quality that is essential to it. But are there included under those two relations all the cases in which we are justified in asking why? If I ask: Why are the three sides of this triangle equal? the answer is: Because the three angles are equal. Now is the equality of the angles the *cause* of the equality of the sides? No, for here it is not a question of any change and thus of any effect that would have to have a cause. Is it merely a ground or reason of knowledge? No, for the equality of the angles is not merely a proof of the equality of the sides, not merely the ground or reason of a judgement; in fact from mere concepts we could never see that, because the angles are equal the sides must also be equal, for the concept of equality of the sides is not contained in that of equality of angles. Here, therefore, it is a connexion not between concepts or judgements, but between sides and angles. The equality of the angles is not the *direct*, but only the *indirect*, reason for *knowing* the equality of the sides, since it is the ground or reason for a thing *to be such as it is* (here for the sides to be equal); thus the angles being equal the sides must be equal. Here we find a necessary connexion between angles and sides, not directly a necessary one between two judgements. Or again, if I ask why *infecta facta*, but never *facta infecta fieri possunt*,[1] hence why the past is absolutely irrevocable, and the future is certain and inevitable, this too cannot be demonstrated in a purely logical way by means of mere concepts; nor is it just a question of causality, for this rules only *events* in time, not time itself. The present hour has hurled the previous one into the bottomless abyss of the past and has forever reduced it to nothing not through causality, but directly through its mere existence itself, yet the taking place of this was inevitable. It is impossible to make this plainer or more intelligible from mere concepts; on the contrary, we recognize it immediately and intuitively just as we do the difference between right and left and all that depends thereon, for example that the left glove does not fit the right hand.

Now as it is not possible to reduce to logical ground

and consequent and to cause and effect all the cases in which the principle of sufficient reason can be applied, it must be that in this classification the law of specification has not been complied with. The law of homogeneity, however, compels us to assume that those cases cannot differ to infinity, but must be reduced to certain species.

Now as it is not possible to reduce to logical ground and consequent and to cause and effect all the cases in which the principle of sufficient reason can be applied, it must be that in this classification the law of specification has not been complied with. The law of homogeneity, however, compels us to assume that those cases cannot differ to infinity, but must be reduced to certain species. Now before I attempt this classification, it is necessary to determine what in all cases is peculiar to the principle of sufficient reason as its special characteristic since the concept of the genus must be settled before those of the species.

§ 16. The Root of the Principle of Sufficient Reason

Our knowing consciousness, appearing as outer and inner sensibility (receptivity), as understanding and as faculty of reason (Vernunft), is divisible into subject and object, and contains nothing else. To be object for the subject and to be our representation or mental picture are the same thing. All our representations are objects of the

41

*subject, and all objects of the subject are our representa-
tions. Now it is found that all our representations stand to
one another in a natural and regular connexion that in form
is determinable A PRIORI. By virtue of this connexion
nothing existing by itself and independent, and also nothing
single and detached, can become an object for us.* It is this
connexion which is expressed by the principle of sufficient
reason in its universality. Now although, as we can infer
from what was previously said, this connexion assumes
different forms according to the difference in the nature of
the objects, such forms being then expressed by a further
modification of the principle of sufficient reason, the
connexion is still always left with that which is common to
all those forms and is expressed in a general and abstract
way by our principle. Therefore the relations, forming the
basis of the principle and to be demonstrated in more detail
in what follows, are what I have called the root of the
principle of sufficient reason. Now on closer consideration
in accordance with the laws of homogeneity and specification, these relations are separated into definite species that
are very different from one another. Their number can be
reduced to *four*, since it agrees with *four classes* into which
everything is divided that can for us become an object, thus
all our representations. These classes are stated and discussed in the four chapters that follow.

In each of them we shall see the principle of sufficient
reason appear in a different form; yet we shall see it
everywhere show itself, by its admitting the above-
mentioned expression, to be the same principle and as
having sprung from the root that is stated here.

Footnotes

1. "What is undone can be done, but what is done can never be undone." [Tr.]

CHAPTER IV

ON THE FIRST CLASS OF OBJECTS FOR THE SUBJECT AND THE FORM OF THE PRINCIPLE OF SUFFICIENT REASON RULING THEREIN

§ 17. General Explanation of This Class of Objects

The first class of possible objects of our faculty of representation is that of *intuitive, perceptive, complete, empirical* representations. They are *intuitive or perceptive* as opposed to concepts that are merely thought and thus are abstract. They are *complete* insofar as they contain, according to Kant's distinction, not merely what is formal, but also what is material in phenomena. They are *empirical* insofar as they proceed not from a mere connexion of ideas, but have their origin in a stimulation of feeling or sensation in our sensitive body to which they constantly refer for evidence as to their reality; and because they are connected, according to the united laws of space, time, and causality, to that endless and beginningless complex that constitutes our *empirical reality*. As, however, according to the result of Kant's teaching, this *empirical reality* does not do away with their *transcendental ideality*, they are here considered merely as representations, where it is a question of the formal elements of knowledge.

§ 18. Outline of a Transcendental Analysis
of Empirical Reality

The forms of these representations are those of the inner and outer senses, namely *time* and *space*; but only as *filled* are these *perceivable*. Their *perceivability* is *matter*, to which I shall return later as well as in § 21.

If time were the only form of these representations, there would be no *coexistence* and therefore nothing *permanent* and no *duration*. For *time* is perceived only insofar as it is filled, and its course is perceived only through the *change* of that which fills it. Therefore an object's *permanence* is recognized only by contrast with the *change* occurring in other objects that exist *simultaneously* with it. But the representation of *coexistence* is not possible in mere time; it depends for its other half on the representation of *space*, because in mere time everything is *successive*, whereas in *space* all things are *side by side*. Therefore the representation of coexistence arises first through the union of time and space.

If, on the other hand, space were the only form of representations of this class, there would be no *change*; for alteration or change is *succession* of states, and *succession is* possible only in *time*. Therefore time can also be defined as the possibility of opposite conditions in the same thing.

Thus we see that although, as is well known, the two forms of empirical representations have in common infinite divisibility and infinite extension, they are nevertheless fundamentally different. And so what is essential to the *one*

46

understanding produces the union between the coexistence of space & time which each by themselves would be meaningless

form has absolutely no meaning in the *other*; juxtaposition has no meaning in time, succession none in space. But the empirical representations, belonging to the ordered and regulated complex of reality, appear in both forms simulta- *space* neously; in fact an *intimate union* of the two is the *&* condition of reality. To a certain extent reality grows out of them as a product out of its factors. What produces this *time* union is the understanding which, by means of its own peculiar function, combines those heterogeneous forms of sensibility so that from their mutual interpenetration, although only for the understanding itself, there arises *empirical reality* as a general and comprehensive representation. This creates a complex, held together by the forms of the principle of sufficient reason, yet with problematical limits. All the individual representations belonging to this class are parts of this complex, and occupy their places therein according to definite laws that are known to us a priori. Thus in the complex innumerable objects exist *simultaneously* because substance, i.e., matter, persists in it despite the irresistible course of time, and because their states change despite the rigid immobility of space. Thus in a word, this entire, objective, real world exists for us in this complex. The reader interested in this will find a more detailed discussion of the analysis of empirical reality, here given only in outline, in the *World as Will and Representation*, Vol. I, § 4. In that work a more detailed explanation is given of the way in which that union, and with it the world of experience, are brought about through the function of the understanding. In Volume II, Chapter 4 of the same work he will also find as

this combination produces an empirical reality as a representation

a supplement the table *Praedicabilia a priori* of Time, Space, and Matter. I recommend it for his careful study, as it will be of great assistance to him; for it shows with special clearness how the contrasts of space and time counterbalance each other in matter as their product which manifests itself in the form of causality.

The function of the understanding, which constitutes the basis of empirical reality, is now to be explained and discussed in detail; only we must first remove by a few incidental remarks the more immediate difficulties which might be encountered by the fundamental idealistic point of view which is here observed.

[handwritten marginalia: Idealism nothing can be known except minds]

§ 19. Immediate Presence of Representations

Now despite this union of the forms of the inner and outer senses through the understanding for the representation of matter, and also for the representation of a permanent external world, the subject has *immediate* knowledge only through the *inner sense*, since the outer is again object of the inner, and the latter again perceives the perceptions of the former. Therefore with regard to the *immediate presence* of representations in its consciousness, the subject remains under the conditions of *time* alone as the form of the *inner sense*.[1] It follows from all this that only *one* distinct representation can be present to the subject at any one time, although such a representation

The outer perceives the representation of the inner sense

may be very complex. (Representation) are *immediately present* implies that they not only become the complete and comprehensive representations of empirical reality in the union of time and space effected by the understanding (which is an intuitive faculty as we shall see in a moment), but are known as representations of the inner sense in mere time, and indeed at the neutral point between the two diverging directions of these, which is called the *present*. The necessary condition, touched on in the previous paragraph, for the immediate presence of a representation of this class is its causal action on our senses and thus on our body, which itself belongs to the objects of this class, and is therefore liable to the law of causality ruling therein and now about to be discussed. For this reason, according to the laws of the inner as well as of the outer world, the subject cannot stop short at that one representation; however, in mere time there is no coexistence. Thus that representation will always vanish again, replaced by others according to an order not determinable a priori but dependent on circumstances shortly to be mentioned. Moreover, it is a well-known fact, not relevant here but to empirical psychology, that the imagination and the dream reproduce the immediate presence of representations. Now despite this transitory and isolated nature of representations with regard to their immediate presence in the consciousness of the subject, there yet remains for the subject, through the function of the understanding, the representation of an all-comprehensive complex of reality, as I have previously described. And so in regard to this antithesis, representations, insofar as they belong to that

49

realism - the attempt to see things as they are w/o idealization

complex, have been looked upon as something quite different from what they are insofar as they are immediately present to consciousness; in the former capacity they are called *real things*, but only in the latter are they called representations "par excellence." [Tr.] [2] This view of the matter, which is the common one, is known by the name of *realism.* With the appearance of modern philosophy *idealism* was opposed to *realism*, and gained more and more ground. Its first representatives were Malebranche and Berkeley, and it was raised by Kant to transcendental idealism, by which the coexistence of the empirical reality of things with their transcendental ideality becomes conceivable. Accordingly, Kant expresses himself as follows in the *Critique of Pure Reason*: "By transcendental idealism of all phenomena I understand that system or doctrine according to which we regard them collectively as mere representations, and not as 'things-in-themselves'." Again in the note: "Space itself is nothing but representation; consequently what is in space must be contained in the representation, and in space there is absolutely nothing except insofar as it is actually represented in it." (Criticism of the Fourth Paralogism of Transcendental Psychology, pp. 369 and 375 of the first edition.) Finally in the "Observation" to this chapter it says: "If I take away the thinking subject, the whole material world must vanish, as this world is nothing but the phenomenal appearance in the sensibility of our own subject, and is a species of this subject's representations." In India idealism is the doctrine even of popular religion, not merely of Brahmanism, but also of Buddhism; only in Europe is it paradoxical in

Is of world is produced by our transcendental identity apperception

Das Ding an Sich. not knowable to consciousness

Kant - our perceptions are organized by the a priori perceptions of space and time and by the categories of understanding

consequence of the essentially and inevitably realistic fundamental view of Judaism. Realism, however, overlooks the fact that the so-called existence of these real things is *absolutely nothing but their being represented* (*Vorgestelltwerden*), or, if it be insisted, only the immediate presence in the consciousness of the subject is to be called being represented "actually" [Tr.][3] or even merely an ability to be represented "potentially." [Tr.][4] Realism overlooks the fact that, outside its reference to the subject, the object no longer remains object, and that, if we take away this reference from the object or abstract from it, then all objective existence is at once abolished. While Leibniz clearly felt that the object is conditioned by the subject, he was yet unable to get rid of the idea of objects existing by themselves, independently of their reference to the subject, that is, independently of their *being represented*. In the first place he assumed a world of objects in themselves which is exactly like, and runs parallel to, the world of the representation, and yet is connected therewith not directly, but only outwardly by means of a *harmonia praestabilita*.[5] This is obviously the most superfluous thing on earth, for it itself never enters perception, and the exactly similar world of the representation pursues its own course without it. When, however, he again tried to determine more closely the essence of things objectively existing in themselves, he found it necessary to declare the objects in themselves to be subjects (*monades*). In this way he gave the most striking proof of the inability of our consciousness, insofar as it is merely cognitive and hence within the limits of the intellect, in other words, of the apparatus for the world of

Criticism of realism

IDEALISM — BUDDHISM
BRAHMANISM
JUDAISM

51

the representation, to find anything beyond subject and
object, representer and representation. Therefore if we
abstract from an object's objectivity (from its being
represented), in other words, if we do away with it as such,
and yet try to assume something, we cannot possibly meet
with anything but the subject. Conversely, if we try to
abstract from the subjectivity of *the subject*, and yet to
have something over, we then have the opposite case which
develops into materialism.

Spinoza had never really got to the bottom of the matter, and had therefore never acquired a clear notion of it; yet
he understood quite well the necessary relation between object and subject as so essential to them that it is the very
condition of our ability to conceive them. He therefore
described it as an identity in the substance (which alone
exists) of that which knows and of that which is extended.

> *Observation:* With reference to the main discussion of this
> paragraph, I take the opportunity to remark that if in the
> course of this essay I make use of the expression *real objects*
> for the sake of brevity and clearness, I understand by this
> nothing but just the representations of intuitive perception
> which are united to form the complex of empirical reality,
> such reality in itself always remaining ideal.

§ 20. Principle of Sufficient Reason of Becoming

In the class of objects for the subject we are now
discussing, the principle of sufficient reason appears as the

law of causality, and I call it as such the *principle of sufficient reason or ground of becoming, principium rationis sufficientis fiendi.* Through it are mutually connected all the objects presenting themselves in the entire general representation, which constitutes the complex of the reality of experience, as regards the appearance and disappearance of their states and hence in the direction of the current of time. The principle is that, if a new state of one or several real objects appears, another state must have preceded it upon which the new state follows regularly, in other words, as often as the first state exists. Such a following is called *ensuing or resulting*; the first state is called the *cause,* the second the *effect.* For example, if a body ignites, this state of burning must have been preceded by a state (1) of affinity for oxygen; (2) of contact with oxygen; (3) of a definite temperature. As soon as this state existed, the ignition was bound to ensue immediately, but only at this moment did it ensue. Therefore that state cannot have existed always, but must have appeared only at this moment. This appearance is called a *change.* Therefore the law of causality is related exclusively to *changes* and is always concerned solely with these. When every effect appears, it is a *change,* and just because it did not appear earlier, it infallibly indicates another *change* that preceded it. In reference to it, this *change* is called *cause,* but in reference to a third *change,* again necessarily preceding it, that same change is called *effect.* This is the chain of causality; it is necessarily without beginning. Accordingly, every state that appears must have ensued or resulted from a change that preceded it. For example, in the case just

53

mentioned, free heat was applied to the body from which a raising of the temperature was bound to ensue. Again, this addition of heat is conditioned by a preceding change, e.g., the falling of the sun's rays on a burning-mirror; this again perhaps by the disappearance of a cloud from where the sun is shining; this again through wind; this wind through the unequal density of the atmosphere; this circumstance through other states and conditions, and so on ad infinitum. If a state contains all the determining factors except one in order to condition the appearance of a new state, then, when *this one* ultimately appears, it will be called the cause "par excellence." [Tr.]⁶ This, of course, is correct insofar as we keep to the final change which is certainly decisive here. Apart from this, however, a determining factor of the causal state has no advantage over others for establishing a causal connexion of things in general, merely because it happens to be the last to appear. Thus in the example just mentioned the removal of the cloud can be called the cause of the ignition insofar as it occurs after the burning-mirror's application to the object. But this could have happened after the disappearance of the cloud, and again the addition of oxygen might have occurred even later. In this respect such accidental determinations of time have to decide which is the cause. On the other hand, if we consider the matter more closely, we find that the *entire state* is the cause of the one that follows. Here it is essentially a matter of indifference in what chronological order its determining factors have come together. Therefore as regards a given individual case, the determining and ultimately appearing factor of a state may be called the cause Κατ᾽ἐξοχήν because it completes the number of the requisite conditions and thus its appearance here becomes the decisive change. Yet for general consideration only the *entire* state, leading to the appearance of the one that follows, can be regarded as cause. The different individual determining factors, however, which, taken together, complete and constitute the cause, can be called the causal moments or elements, or even the *conditions*, and accordingly the cause can be split up into these. On the other hand, it is quite wrong to call the objects, and not the state, the cause; for example, in the above-mentioned case, some would call the burning-mirror the cause of the ignition, others the cloud, others again the sun, or the oxygen, and so on arbitrarily and without order. But there is absolutely no sense in saying that one object is the cause of another, first because objects contain not merely form and quality, but also *matter* which does not arise or pass away; and then because the law of causality refers exclusively to *changes*, in other words, to the appearance and disappearance of states in time. Here it regulates that relation in reference whereof the earlier state is called the *cause*, the later the *effect*, and their necessary connexion the *resulting or ensuing* of the one from the other.

Here I refer the attentive reader to the explanations given in my *World as Will and Representation*, Vol. II, Chap. 4. For it is of the highest importance for us to have perfectly clear and fixed ideas of the true and real significance of the law of causality, and also of the sphere of its validity. Hence it is most important for us clearly to recognize first and foremost that the law of causality relates solely and exclusively to *changes* of material states, and to nothing else whatever. Consequently, it must not be introduced when *these* are not mentioned. Thus the law of causality is the regulator of the *changes* undergone in time by objects of external *experience*; but all these are material. Every change can take place only through another having preceded it, which is determined according to a rule, but by which it then takes place as having been necessarily brought about. This necessity is the causal nexus.

Accordingly, simple as the law of causality is, we yet find it, as a rule, expressed quite differently in philosophical manuals from the earliest to the most modern times, namely in more abstract, and thus broader and less definite, terms. It says, for instance, that a cause is that by which something else comes into existence, or that which produces another thing, or actually makes it, and so on; thus Wolff says: "The cause is the principle on which the existence or actuality of another entity depends"; [Tr.] [7] whereas with causality we are obviously concerned only with changes in the form of indestructible matter that is without origin, and a real genesis, a coming into existence, of that which previously never existed, is an impossibility. Now it is true that vagueness and confusion of thought may in most cases be responsible for those conventional, wide, distorted, and false conceptions of the causal relation. But sometimes there is certainly behind this an intention, namely a theological flirting from a distance with the cosmological proof. To satisfy this, it is ready to falsify even transcendental a priori truths (this mother's milk of the human understanding). We have the clearest instance of this in Thomas Brown's book *On the Relation of Cause and Effect*. Running to 460 pages, it had already reached its fourth edition in 1835, and probably has since gone through several more. Apart from its tedious, pedantic, and rambling prolixity, it does not handle its subject badly. Now this Englishman quite rightly recognized that it is always *changes* with which the law of causality is concerned, and that every effect is therefore a *change*. Yet although it cannot possibly have escaped his notice, he will not admit that a cause is likewise a *change* from which it follows that the whole thing is merely the uninterrupted nexus of *changes* succeeding one another in time. On the contrary, with extreme ineptitude, he always calls the cause an *object* that *precedes* the change, or even substance. With this utterly false expression which always mars his explanations, he turns and twists pitiably throughout his long book against his better knowledge and *conscience*. This he does simply in order that his statement may not stand in the way of the cosmological proof that some day is to be given elsewhere and by others. But what must be the state of a truth for which the way has to be paved from a distance and by such tricks?

But what have our own worthy, honest German professors of philosophy done on their part for their dear cosmological proof, that is to say, after Kant had dealt it a mortal blow in his *Critique of Pure Reason*—they who value intellect and truth above all else? It was of course a critical situation, for (as these worthies know although they do not say so) *causa prima* is, just like *causa sui*, a *contradictio in adjecto*,[8] although the former expression is much more

57

often used than the latter. Moreover, it is usually pronounced with quite a serious and even solemn air; indeed many men, especially English reverends, roll their eyes in a really edifying manner when they express with emphasis and emotion that *contradictio in adjecto*,[8] the first cause. They know that a first cause is just as inconceivable as is the point where space has an end or as the moment when time had a beginning. For every cause is a *change*, and here we are necessarily bound to ask about the change which preceded it, and by which it had been brought about, and so on ad infinitum, ad infinitum! Not even a first state of matter is conceivable from which, as it never yet exists, all subsequent states could have proceeded. For if in itself it had been their cause, they too would have had to exist from all eternity, and hence the present state would not be only at this moment. But if that first state began to be causal only at a certain time, then something must have *changed* it at that time for its inactivity to have ceased. But then something came about, a change occurred, and we must at once ask about its cause, in other words, about a change that preceded *it*, and we again find ourselves on the ladder of causes up which we are whipped by the inexorable law of causality higher and higher, ad infinitum, ad infinitum. (These gentlemen will surely not have the effrontery to speak to me about matter itself arising out of nothing. If so, there are corollaries later on at their service.) The law of causality is therefore not so obliging as to allow itself to be used like a cab which we dismiss after we reach our destination. On the contrary, it is like the broom that is brought to life by Goethe's apprentice magician;[9] when

once it is set in motion, it will not stop running and
fetching water, so that only the old wizard himself can
bring it to rest. But these gentlemen are not all master
wizards. And so what did they do, these noble and sincere
friends of truth, who in their profession are always waiting
only for merit in order to proclaim it to the world as soon
as it shows itself, and who, far from wishing to suppress by
cunning silence and cowardly secreting the works of anyone
coming along and actually being what they only imagine
they are, will rather be at once the proclaimers of his merit,
as surely and certainly as folly loves wisdom above all else?
What did they do for their old friend, the hard-pressed and
prostrate cosmological proof? They thought of a clever
ruse. "Friend," they said, "you are in a bad way, really bad,
since your fatal encounter with that stubborn old man of
Königsberg; indeed you are as badly off as your brothers,
the ontological and physico-theological proofs. But be of
good cheer, *we* shall not abandon you (we are paid for this,
you know). However, you must change your name and
clothes,—there is no option; for if we call you by your
proper name, everyone will take to his heels. But incognito
we take you by the arm and again introduce you to people
only, as we have said, it must be incognito. Then everything
will be all right! First of all, your theme will now have the
name of 'the Absolute'; this has a foreign, decent, and
aristocratic ring; and we know best what can be done with
Germans by assuming an air of superiority. Everyone, of
course, understands what is meant and thus thinks he is a
sage. You yourself, however, appear disguised in the form
of an enthymeme.[10] Be sure to leave behind all your

Exhortations to philosophers

prosyllogisms[10] and premisses with which you used to drag us up the long climax, for everyone knows that they are quite useless. Appear as a man of few words, with a proud, bold, and superior air, and at one bound you will reach the goal. You shout (and we accompany you): 'The Absolute, confound it, _this must exist_, otherwise there would be nothing at all!' (With this you bang the table.) But where does this come from? 'Silly question! Haven't I said that it was the Absolute?' That will do, upon my soul, that will do! The Germans are accustomed to accept words instead of ideas. Are they not trained by us for this purpose from early youth? Just look at Hegelry; what is it but empty, hollow, and even nauseous verbiage? And yet how brilliant was the career of this philosophical creature of the ministry! It needed only a few mercenary fellows to sing the praises of the bad, and their voices found an echo in the hollow emptiness of a thousand numbskulls, an echo resounding and spreading even at the present time. See how soon a great philosopher was made from a common head, indeed from a common charlatan! Have courage, therefore! Moreover, friend and patron, we second you even in other ways; indeed we cannot live without you! If that carping old critic of Königsberg has criticized reason and clipped _her_ wings,—well then we shall invent a _new_ reason of which no one had ever heard anything. It will be a reason that does not think but has direct _intuition_, that perceives _ideas_ (a high-flown word made to mystify) real and embodied or even _apprehends_ them, directly apprehends what you and others first wanted to prove; or again a reason that _divines or surmises_, namely with those who admit only a little but

He hates Hegel

who are also content therewith. We thus pass off early inculcated popular conceptions as direct inspirations of this new reason of ours, indeed as inspirations from above. We degrade the old reason that was driven out by criticism, call it *understanding*, and send it about its business. And as regards the true understanding proper,—well, what in all the world is it to us? You smile incredibly, but we know our public and the *harum horum*[11] we have before us on the students' benches. Bacon said: "Young men learn to believe at universities." For they can learn from us something really good; we have in stock a good supply of articles of faith. If you feel nervous, always bear in mind that we are in Germany where men have been able to do what would have been impossible elsewhere. I refer to the fact that in Germany men proclaim as a great mind and profound thinker a dull, ignorant philosophaster, a scribbler of nonsense, who by his ineffably hollow verbiage thoroughly and permanently disorganizes their brains; I refer to our dearly beloved Hegel. Not only have they been able to do this with impunity and without incurring ridicule, but they have believed it for the last thirty years, and believe it even to this day! Therefore if only we have the Absolute with your help, we are safe, in spite of Kant and his *Critique*. We then philosophize condescendingly, make the world pro- *critique* ceed from the Absolute by means of the most varied deductions that resemble one another only by their tormenting tedium. We call the world the finite and the Absolute the infinite,—again this gives us an agreeable variation in our idle display of words. In general we speak always only of God, explain how, why, for what purpose, for what reason, by what voluntary or involuntary process he created or produced the world, whether he is without or within, and so forth, as though philosophy were theology, and looked for enlightenment not on the world but on God."

Therefore the cosmological proof, to which the above apostrophe was addressed and with which we are here concerned, really consists in the assertion that the principle of reason or ground of becoming or the law of causality necessarily leads to an idea by which the law itself is abolished and is declared null and void. For we reach the *causa prima* (the Absolute) only by ascending from consequent to ground or reason through a series of any length we like; but we cannot stop short of it without annulling the principle of sufficient reason.

After briefly and clearly showing the invalid nature of the cosmological proof, as I had in the case of the ontological in the second chapter, I shall probably be asked by the interested reader to do also what is necessary as regards the physico-theological proof which is much more plausible. But here it is wholly out of place, as its subject-matter belongs to quite a different branch of philosophy. In the connexion I therefore refer him to Kant's *Critique of Pure Reason,* and also *ex professo*[12] to his *Critique of Judgement.* As a supplement to Kant's purely negative method I refer also to my position in the *Will in Nature*, a work small in volume but rich and weighty in content. On the other hand, the reader not interested can pass on intact to his descendants this and indeed all my works. It matters not to me since I am here not for one generation but for many.

As will be shown in § 21, the law of causality is known to us a priori and is therefore transcendental, valid for every possible experience, and consequently without exception. Moreover, this law establishes that on a definitely given, relatively first state, a second equally definite state must ensue according to a rule, in other words, at all times. Therefore the relation between cause and effect is a necessary one, so that the law of causality authorizes us to form hypothetical judgements. In this way it shows itself to be a form of the principle of sufficient reason on which all hypothetical judgements must rest and all *necessity* is based, as will be shown later on.

I call this form of our principle the principle of sufficient reason of *becoming* because its application invariably presupposes a change, the appearance of a new state and hence a becoming (*ein Werden*). Moreover, one of its essential characteristics is that the cause always precedes the effect in time (compare § 47), and only from this do we know originally which of two states, united by the causal nexus, is cause and which effect. Conversely, there are cases where from previous experience the causal nexus is known to us, but the succession of states follows so rapidly that it escapes our observation. From causality we then infer the succession with absolute certainty, for example that the ignition of the powder precedes the explosion. In this connexion I refer to the *World as Will and Representation*, Vol. II, Chap. 4.

Again from this essential connexion between causality and succession, it follows that the concept of *reciprocal effect* or *reciprocity* has strictly speaking no meaning. Thus it presupposes that the effect is again the cause of its cause and hence that what follows was at the same time what precedes. I have shown at length the inadmissibility of this favourite concept in my Criticism of the Kantian Philosophy which forms an appendix to the first volume of the *World as Will and Representation*, and so to this I refer the reader. It is observed that authors as a rule make use of this concept when their insight becomes less clear, and so this accounts for its frequent use. In fact, when a writer comes to the end of his conceptions, no word suggests itself more readily than "reciprocity." Therefore the reader may regard it even as a kind of alarm gun, indicating that the author has got out of his depth. It is also worth noting that the word *Wechselwirkung* (reciprocal effect or action) is found only in German, and that no other language possesses an ordinary everyday equivalent thereof.

Two important *corollaries* result from the law of causality, and, because of this, are accredited as knowledge *a priori* and consequently as beyond all doubt and without exception. They are the *law of inertia* and the law of the *permanence of substance*. The first implies that every state, consequently a body's state of rest as well as its motion of any kind, must continue and even last throughout endless time without change, increase, or diminution, unless a cause supervenes which alters or abolishes it. But the other law expressing the eternity of matter follows from the fact that the law of causality refers only to the *states* of bodies, and hence to their rest, motion, form, and quality, since it governs their arising and passing away in time. On the other

2 corollaries of the law of causality
1 law of inertia
2 " " permanence of substance (matter)

In beer drinking what about brain cell destruction? (if true)

hand, it is by no means related to the existence of *that which bears* these states, and has been given the name *substance*, simply to express its exemption from all arising and passing away. *Substance is permanent*, in other words, it cannot arise or pass away; consequently, the quantity thereof existing in the world can never be increased or diminished. This we know a priori, as is testified by the consciousness of the unshakable certainty with which everyone who has seen a given body disappear, whether by sleight of hand, analysis, combustion, evaporation, or by any other process, nevertheless firmly assumes that, whatever the body's *form* may have become, its substance, i.e., its *matter*, must exist and be found somewhere. In the same way we know that, whenever we come across a body that did not previously exist, it must have been brought there, or have assumed a concrete form from invisible particles, possibly through precipitation. But we never assert as regards its substance (matter) that it could have come into existence, for this implies an utter impossibility and is absolutely inconceivable. The certainty with which we state this in advance (a priori) springs from the fact that our understanding possesses absolutely no form for conceiving an arising or passing away of matter. For the law of causality, the only form under which we are able to conceive changes at all, always concerns merely the *states* of bodies, never the existence of that which *bears or carries* all states, namely *matter*. I therefore lay down the principle of the permanence of substance as a corollary of the law of causality. Moreover, we cannot possibly have arrived a posteriori at the conviction of the permanence of substance, because in most cases it is impossible to verify the facts empirically, and also because every piece of empirical knowledge, obtained merely by induction, has always only approximate and hence precarious, never absolute, certainty. Therefore the certainty of our conviction as regards that principle is of quite a different nature and species from that concerning the accuracy of some *empirically* discovered natural law, since it has an entirely different, perfectly unshakable, and never wavering firmness. This is because that principle expresses *transcendental* knowledge, that is, a knowledge that determines and fixes *prior* to all experience everything possible in all experience. But in this very way, such knowledge reduces the world of experience generally to a mere phenomenon of the brain. Even the most universal of all the different kinds of natural laws, and the one liable to the least exception, namely the law of gravitation, is of empirical origin and hence without guarantee as to its absolute universality. Therefore it is still called in question from time to time; moreover, doubts occasionally arise as to its validity even beyond the solar system. In fact astronomers are careful to emphasize indications and corroborations of this, whenever they find them, thereby making it clear that they regard it as merely empirical. The question can, of course, be raised whether gravitation occurs even between bodies separated by an *absolute* vacuum; or whether it is brought about inside a solar system, possibly by means of an ether, and so might not operate between fixed stars; but then only empirically can such questions be decided. This proves that here we are not concerned with any a priori knowledge. On the other hand, if we assume as most probable that every solar system has been formed through the gradual condensation of a primary and original nebula according to the hypothesis of Kant and Laplace, we still cannot for one moment conceive that primary substance as having originated from *nothing.* On the contrary, we are compelled to assume that its particles had previously existed somewhere, and had merely been brought together, just because the principle of the permanence of substance is transcendental. In my "Criticism of the Kantian Philosophy" (see my chief work, Volume I, Appendix), I have shown in detail that *substance* is a mere synonym of *matter*, because the concept of substance is realizable only in matter and thus originates therefrom; and I have specially pointed out how that concept was formed merely for a surreptitious purpose. Like many other equally certain truths, this a priori certain eternity of matter (called permanence of substance) is for the professors of philosophy forbidden fruit; and so they slip past it with a bashful side-glance.

Two things remain untouched by the endless chain of causes and effects which directs all *changes* but never extends beyond these, and precisely on this account they remain untouched. They are *matter*, as I have just shown, and the original *forces of nature*. Matter remains untouched because it is the *bearer* of all changes or that *in which* such changes occur. The primary forces of nature are not touched because they are that *by virtue of which* changes or effects are at all possible, that which first gives to causes their causality, i.e., the ability to act, and hence that by which the causes hold this ability merely in fee. Cause and

2 things untouched by C/E's
67
① matter
② forces of nature

effect are the *changes* bound to necessary succession in time; the forces of nature, on the other hand, by virtue of which all causes operate, are excluded from all change. Therefore in this sense they are outside all time, but precisely on that account exist always and everywhere, are omnipresent and inexhaustible, and are ever-ready to manifest themselves as soon as an opportunity presents itself on the guiding line of causality. The cause, like its effect, is always something individual, a single change; the force of nature, on the other hand, is something universal, unchangeable, and existing always and everywhere. For example, the attraction of the thread by the amber at this moment is the effect; its cause is the preceding friction and the present proximity of the amber, and the *force of nature*, acting in and presiding over this process, is electricity. The explanation of all this is found in a detailed example in the *World as Will and Representation*, Vol. I, § 26. I have there shown in a long chain of causes and effects how the most heterogeneous forces of nature successively appear in them and come into play. In this way, the difference between cause and natural force, between the fleeting phenomenon and the eternal form of activity, becomes exceedingly clear. In that work the whole of § 26 is devoted to this investigation, and so it suffices here merely to state the case briefly. The *norm* or *rule*, observed by a force of nature in regard to its *appearance* in the chain of causes and effects, and hence the bond connecting it with this, is the *law of nature*. But the confusion of natural force with cause is as frequent as it is detrimental to a clearness of thought. Indeed, it appears as if, prior to me, these concepts had never been properly separated, however great the necessity for this may have been. Not only are natural forces themselves turned into causes, by our saying that electricity, gravitation, and so on are the cause, but they are even turned into effects by many who ask for a cause of electricity, gravitation, and so on, which is absurd. But it is something quite different when we diminish the number of natural forces by reducing one of them to another, as magnetism is to electricity at the present time. Every *genuine*, and thus actually original, force of nature, however, and this also includes every fundamental chemical property, is essentially a *qualitas occulta*, that is to say, it is no longer capable of a physical, but only of a metaphysical, explanation, in other words, of one that transcends the phenomenon. No one has carried this confusion, or rather identification, of natural force with cause so far as Maine de Biran has in his *Nouvelles considérations des rapports du physique au moral*, since this is essential to his philosophy. In this connexion it is remarkable that, when he speaks of causes, he hardly ever puts *cause* alone, but almost always says *cause ou force*,[13] just as we previously saw in § 8 how Spinoza wrote *ratio sive causa* eight times on the same page. Thus both are conscious of identifying two disparate concepts in order to be able to make use of either of them according to the circumstances. Now for this purpose they are compelled always to keep the identification present in the reader's mind.

Thus causality, this director of each and every change, now appears in nature in *three* different forms, namely as cause in the narrowest sense, as *stimulus*, and as *motive*. It is precisely on this difference that the true and essential distinction is based between inorganic bodies, plants, and animals, and not on external anatomical, or even chemical characteristics.

The cause in the narrowest sense is that according to which alone changes ensue in the *inorganic* kingdom, namely those effects that are the theme of mechanics, physics, and chemistry. Newton's third fundamental law: "Action and reaction are equal to each other," applies exclusively to cause, and says that the preceding state (the cause) undergoes a change which in magnitude equals the change (the effect) brought about by that state. Further, it is only in this form of causality that the degree of the effect always corresponds exactly to that of the cause, so that the one can be calculated from the other.

The second form of causality is the *stimulus*; it governs organic life as such and hence the life of plants, and the vegetative and thus unconscious part of animal life, which is in fact just a plant life. This second form is characterized by the absence of the distinctive signs of the first. Thus here action and reaction are not equal to each other, and the intensity of the effect through all its degrees by no means corresponds to the intensity of the cause; on the contrary, by intensifying the cause the effect may even be turned into its opposite.

The third form of causality is the *motive*. In this form causality controls animal life proper and hence *conduct*, that is, the external, consciously performed actions of all animals. The medium of motives is *knowledge*; consequently susceptibility to motives requires an intellect. Therefore knowing, the forming of a representation or mental picture, is the true characteristic of the animal. As such the animal always moves towards an aim and end; accordingly this must have been *known or recognized* by the animal, that is to say, it must present itself to him as something different from himself, yet as that of which he is conscious. Accordingly, the animal can be defined as "that which knows"; no other definition quite hits the mark, indeed it is possible that no other could stand the test. An absence of knowledge necessarily implies also an absence of movement on motives; therefore there remains only movement on stimuli, namely plant life; and so irritability and sensibility are inseparable. But a motive's mode of acting is obviously different from that of a stimulus; thus the operation of a motive can be very brief, in fact it need only be momentary; for its effectiveness, unlike that of the stimulus, bears no relation to its duration, to the proximity of the object, and so on. On the contrary, the motive need only be perceived in order to operate, whereas the stimulus always requires contact, often even intussusception, but invariably a certain duration.

This brief statement of the three forms of causality is adequate here. Their detailed discussion will be found in Sec. III of my prize-essay "On the Freedom of the Will" in the *Two Fundamental Problems of Ethics*. Here I will insist only on one point. The difference between cause, stimulus, and motive is obviously only the result of the degree of *receptivity* or *susceptibility* of beings; the greater this is, the lighter can be the mode of operation; thus a stone must be kicked, whereas man obeys a glance. But both are moved by a sufficient cause and hence with equal necessity; for motivation is merely causality passing through knowledge; the intellect is the medium of motives because it is the highest stage of receptivity. But in this way, the law of causality loses absolutely nothing of its rigour, exactness, and certainty. The motive is a cause, and it operates with the necessity entailed by all causes. This necessity is easy to see in the case of the animal whose intellect is simpler and thus furnishes only knowledge of the present. Man's intellect is double; in addition to knowledge of intuitive perception, he has also abstract knowledge, and this is not bound to the present; in other words, he has the faculty of reason (*Vernunft*). He therefore has an elective decision with clear consciousness; thus he can balance mutually exclusive motives as such one against the other, in other words, he can let them try their strength on his will; whereupon the more powerful motive then decides him, and his action ensues with precisely the same necessity with which the rolling of a ball results from its being struck. Freedom of the will[14] means (not the twaddle of professors of philosophy but) "*that two different actions are possible to a given person in a given situation.*" But the utter *absurdity* of this assertion is a truth demonstrated as certainly and as clearly as any truth can be that goes beyond the sphere of pure mathematics. In my prize-essay "On the Freedom of Will" which was awarded a prize by the Royal Norwegian Society of Scientific Studies, the reader will find this truth discussed most clearly, methodically, thoroughly, and moreover with special reference to the facts of self-consciousness, by which ignorant people imagine they have confirmed the above-mentioned absurdity. Generally speaking, however, the same thing has already been taught by Hobbes, Spinoza, Priestly, Voltaire, and even by Kant.[15] Now, of course, this does not prevent our worthy professors of philosophy from talking about the freedom of the will as a settled affair quite ingenuously and as if nothing had happened. For what purpose then do these gentlemen imagine the above-named great men came into existence by the grace of nature? To enable *them* (the professors) to live by philosophy? Now after I had expounded the matter in my prize-essay more clearly than had ever been done before, and moreover with the sanction of a Royal Society which included my work in its archives, it was surely the duty of these gentlemen with their way of thinking to oppose such a pernicious and erroneous doctrine, such a detestable heresy, and thoroughly to refute it. This was the more necessary as in the same volume (*The Two Fundamental Problems of Ethics*), namely in the prize-essay "On the Basis of Morality," I had shown the utter groundlessness and futility of Kant's assumption of practical reason with its categorical imperative, still always used by these gentlemen under the name of "moral law" as the foundation-stone for their shallow systems of morality. I have shown all this so irrefutably and clearly that no one with a spark of judgement can any longer believe in that fiction after he has read it. "Well, they probably have done this!" Oh no! They will take good care not to venture on slippery ground! Maintaining silence and keeping the mouth shut; these constitute their whole talent and sole means

Kant's binding moral law

against intellect, mental powers, seriousness, and truth. In none of the products of their useless scribblings that have appeared since 1841 has a single word been said about my ethics, although it is unquestionably the most important ethical work that has appeared in the last sixty years. Indeed, so great is their fear of me and my truth, that the book has not even been announced in any of the literary journals that are issued by universities or academies. *Zitto, zitto,*[16] lest the public should notice anything; this is and remains their whole policy. Of course, the instinct of self-preservation may be at the bottom of this crafty conduct. For is not a philosophy that is directed to truth and has no other consideration bound to play the role of the iron pot among earthen ones, when it makes its appearance among the petty systems that are framed under the influence of a thousand regards and motives by men thus qualified on account of their way of thinking? Their miserable fear of my works if fear of the truth. For instance the very doctrine of the complete necessity of all the acts of will certainly stands in flagrant contradiction with all the assumptions of their favourite petticoat philosophy that is cut to the pattern of Judaism. But far from being disturbed by such philosophy, this strictly demonstrated truth, as a sure datum and criterion, as a true [saying of Archimedes] "Give me a foothold [and I shall move the earth] ," [Tr.][17] rather proves the futility of that whole petticoat philosophy, and the necessity for a fundamentally different and incomparably deeper view of the nature of the world and of man, no matter whether or not such a view is compatible with the rights and privileges of professors of philosophy.

§ 21. A Priori Nature of the Concept of Causality. Intellectual Nature of Empirical Intuitive Perception. The Understanding

In the professorial philosophy of our philosophy-professors we shall always find that intuitive perception of an external world is the business of the senses, whereupon there follows a lengthy and diffuse dissertation on each of the five senses. On the other hand, there is no mention of the intellectual nature of intuitive perception, namely that it is in the main the work of the understanding. By means of the form of causality peculiar to it, and of time and space, the form of pure sensibility attributed to causality, the understanding first creates and produces this objective external world out of the raw material of a few sensations in the organs of sense. And yet in 1813 I discussed the principal points in the first edition of the present essay, and afterwards in 1816 in my essay *On Vision and Colours,* Professor Rosas of Vienna showed his approval of my discussion in that he was induced thereby to plagiarize. Further details of this are found in *On the Will in Nature*.[18] On the other hand, the professors of philosophy have taken no more notice of this truth than they have of the other great and important truths whose exposition has been the task and toil of my whole life in order that they may become the permanent possession of mankind. This is not to their taste; it does not serve their purpose at all or lead to theology It is certainly not suited to the proper training of students for the highest State posts. In short, the professors do not want to learn anything from me; they do not see how much they would have to learn, namely all that their children and their children's children will learn from me. Instead of this, each sits down to enrich the public with his original ideas in a long spun-out system of metaphysics. If for this fingers are a qualification, then he is qualified. But Machiavelli is quite right when he says, as did Hesiod (Ἔργα, 293) before him: "There are three kinds of minds; first those that acquire insight and an understanding of things from their own resources; then those that recognize what is right when it is pointed out to them by others; and finally those that are incapable of doing either the one or the other." (*Il Principe*, c. 22.)

One must be forsaken by all the gods to imagine that the world of intuitive perception outside, filling space in its three dimensions, moving on in the inexorably strict course of time, governed at each step by the law of causality that is without exception, but in all these respects merely observing laws that we are able to state prior to all experience thereof—that such a world outside had an entirely real and objective existence without our participation, but then found its way into our heads through mere sensation, where it now had a second existence like the one outside. For what a poor, wretched thing mere sensation is! Even in the noblest organs of sense it is nothing more than a local specific feeling, capable in its way of some variation, yet in itself always subjective. Therefore, as such, this feeling cannot possibly contain anything objective, and so anything resembling intuitive perception. For sensation of every kind is and remains an event within the organism itself; but as such it is restricted to the region beneath the skin; and so, in itself, it can never contain anything lying outside the skin and thus outside ourselves. Sensation can be pleasant or unpleasant—and this indicates a reference to our will—but nothing objective is to be found in any sensation. In the organs of sense sensation is heightened by the confluence of the nerve extremities; it can easily be stimulated from without by the wide distribution and thin covering of these; and, moreover, it is specially susceptible to particular influences, such as light, sound, and odour. Yet it remains mere sensation, like every other within our body; consequently, it is something essentially subjective whose changes directly reach our consciousness only in the form of the *inner* sense and hence of time alone, that is to say, successively. It is only when the *understanding* begins to act—a function not of single delicate nerve extremities but of that complex and mysterious structure the brain that weighs three pounds and even five in exceptional cases,— only when the understanding applies its sole form, *the law of causality*, that a powerful transformation takes place whereby subjective sensation becomes objective intuitive perception. Thus by virtue of its own peculiar form and so a priori, in other words, *prior* to all experience (since till then experience was not yet possible), the understanding grasps the given sensation of the body as an *effect* (a word comprehended only by the understanding), and this effect as such must necessarily have a *cause*. Simultaneously the understanding summons to its assistance *space*, the form of the *outer* sense also lying predisposed in the intellect, i.e., in the brain. This it does in order to place that cause

outside the organism; for only in this way does there arise
for it an outside whose possibility is simply space, so that
pure intuition a priori must supply the foundation for
empirical perception. In this process, as I shall soon show in
more detail, the understanding now avails itself of all the
data of the given sensation, even the minutest, in order to
construct in space, in conformity therewith, the *cause* of
the sensation. This operation of the understanding (which,
however, is expressly denied by Schelling in the first
volume of his *Philosophische Schriften* of 1809, pp.
237-38, and likewise by Fries in his *Kritik der Vernunft*,
Vol. I, pp. 52-56 and 290 of the first edition), is not
discursive or reflective, nor does it take place *in abstracto*
by means of concepts and words; on the contrary, it is
intuitive and quite immediate. For only by this operation
and consequently in the understanding and for the understanding does the real, objective, corporeal world, filling
space in three dimensions, present itself; and then it
proceeds, according to the same law of causality, to change
in time and to move in space. Accordingly, the understanding itself has first to create the objective world, for this
cannot just step into our heads from without, already cut
and dried, through the senses and the openings of their
organs. Thus the senses furnish nothing but the raw
material, and this the understanding first of all works up
into the objective grasp and apprehension of a corporeal
world governed by laws, and does so by means of the
simple forms already stated, namely space, time, and
causality. Accordingly, our daily *empirical intuitive perception is intellectual*, and *it* has a right to claim this

78

hearing, smell, taste

predicate, which the philosophical braggarts of Germany have attributed to a pretended intuition of imaginary worlds where their beloved Absolute is supposed to perform its evolutions. But I will now show in more detail first the great gulf between sensation and intuitive perception by pointing out how raw the material is from which the beautiful work arises.

Properly speaking, only two senses, touch and sight, are of use to objective intuitive perception. These alone supply the data, and on their foundation the understanding enables the objective world to come about through the process just mentioned. The other three senses on the whole remain subjective; for it is true that their sensations point to an external cause, but yet contain no data for determining its *spatial* relations. But now *space* is the form of all intuitive perception, i.e., of *that* apprehension in which alone *objects* can, properly speaking, present themselves. Therefore those three senses can, of course, serve to announce to us the presence of objects already known to us in another way; but no spatial construction and thus no objective intuitive perception is brought about on the basis of their data. We can never construct a rose from its perfume, and a blind man can hear music all his life without obtaining the slightest objective representation of the musicians, the instruments, or the vibrations of the air. On the other hand, the sense of hearing is of great value as a medium of language, whereby it is the sense of *reason* or of the *rational* faculty (*Vernunft*), whose name is even derived from it.[19] It is also valuable as a medium of music of the only way to grasp complex numerical relations not merely

touch, sight – objective intuitive perception
other 3 – subjective. their sensations point to an external cause

in abstracto, but immediately and thus *in concreto*. But the
tone never indicates spatial relations, and so never leads us
to the nature of its cause. On the contrary, we stop short at
the tone itself; consequently, it is no datum for the
understanding that is constructing the objective world.
Only the sensations of touch and sight are such data; and
so, of course, a blind man without hands and feet could
construct for himself a priori space in all its conformity to
law, but he would gain only a very indistinct representation
of the objective world. However, what touch and sight
supply is still not by any means intuitive perception, but
only the raw material for this; for perception is so far from
being found in the sensations of these senses that, on the
contrary, they do not resemble at all the qualities of things
presented to us by means of them, as I shall show in a
moment. Here we must clearly separate what actually
belongs to sensation from what the intellect has added in
intuitive perception. At first this is difficult because we are
so accustomed to pass directly from the sensation to its
cause that this presents itself to us without our noticing the
sensation in and by itself which furnishes, so to speak, the
premisses to that conclusion of the understanding.

Therefore touch and sight have in the first instance
their own particular advantages and thus assist each other.
Sight needs no contact or even proximity; its field is
limitless and extends to the stars; moreover, it is sensitive to
the most delicate degrees of light, shade, colour, and
transparency, and hence furnishes the understanding with a
great deal of finely determined data. From these the
understanding by dint of practice constructs and at once

presents in intuitive perception the shape, size, distance, and nature of bodies. On the other hand, it is true that touch is restricted to contact, but its data are so infallible and varied that it is the most radical and thorough sense. Indeed perceptions through sight ultimately refer to touch, and sight can be regarded as an imperfect touch extending to a distance and making use of the rays of light as long feelers. It is therefore exposed to many deceptions just because it is limited entirely to qualities that are brought about through the medium of light; and so it is one-sided. Touch, on the other hand, immediately supplies the data for the knowledge of size, shape, hardness, softness, dryness, moisture, smoothness, temperature, and so on. In this it is assisted by the shape and mobility of the arms, hands, and fingers from whose position the understanding, by touching bodies, derives the data for constructing them in space; it is also aided through muscular power by means whereof it knows the weight, solidity, toughness, or brittleness of bodies; all this with the least possibility of deception.

In spite of all this, these data still do not by any means give us intuitive perception; this remains the work of the understanding. If I press against a table with my hand, the sensation I get certainly does not contain the representation of the firm cohesion of the parts of that mass; indeed it does not contain anything like this. On the contrary, it is only when my understanding passes from the sensation to the cause thereof that it constructs for itself a body having the properties of solidity, impenetrability, and hardness. If in the dark I put my hand on a flat surface, or seize a ball of some three inches in diameter, then in both cases it is the same parts of the hand which feel the pressure. Only from the different position, assumed by my hand in the one case or the other, does my understanding construct the shape of the body, contact with which is the cause of the sensation, and it confirms this sensation for itself by my varying the points of contact. If a man born blind touches a body of cubical shape, the sensations in his hand are quite uniform; they are the same on all sides and in every direction. It is true that the edges press on a smaller part of his hand, yet these sensations contain absolutely nothing resembling a cube. But from the resistance felt, his understanding infers immediately and intuitively a cause thereof, and through that inference the cause now presents itself as a solid body. From the movements of his arms when touching the object, while the sensation of the hands remains the same, he constructs the cubical shape of the body in space which is known to him a priori. If he did not already have within himself the representation of a cause and of a space together with its laws, the image of a cube could never result from those successive sensations in his hand. If we let a rope run through our closed hand, then, as the cause of the friction and of the duration thereof and in this position of our hand, the rope will construct a long cylindrical body moving uniformly in the same direction. But from that mere sensation in his hand there could never come to him the representation of movement, i.e., change of place in space by means of time. For the sensation cannot contain such a thing, nor can it alone ever produce anything resembling this. On the contrary, his intellect must carry within itself, prior to all experience, the intuitions of space, time, and with these that of the possibility of movement; it must likewise contain the representation of causality in order now to pass from sensation, given only empirically, to a cause thereof, and then to construct such a cause as a body of some shape or other, moving in this or that way. For what a difference there is between the mere sensation in my hand and the representation of causality, materiality, and movement in space by means of time! Even if the position and points of contact of my hand were varied, the sensation therein would be something far too uniform and poor in data for me to be able to construct therefrom the representation of space with three dimensions and of the influence of bodies on one another, together with the properties of expansion, impenetrability, cohesion, shape, hardness, softness, rest, and motion, in short, the basis of the objective world. On the contrary, this is possible only by there being preformed in the intellect itself space as the form of intuitive perception, time as the form of change, and the law of causality as the regulator of the appearance of changes. Now it is precisely the existence of these forms, ready-made and prior to all experience, which constitutes the intellect. Physiologically it is function of the brain which learns this just as little from experience as does the stomach to digest or the liver to secrete bile. Only in this way can we explain the fact that many a person born blind acquires so complete a knowledge of the relations of space as to enable him to replace in a high degree his lack of eyesight, and to perform astonishing feats. Thus a hundred years ago Saunderson, who was blind from the cradle, lectured at Cambridge on mathematics, optics, and astronomy. (Diderot in his *Lettre sur les aveugles* gives a detailed account of Saunderson.) And only so can we explain the opposite case of Eva Lauk who, though born without arms and legs, acquired an accurate intuitive perception of the external world by means of sight alone just as rapidly as did other children. (An account of her will be found in the *World as Will and Representation*, Vol. II, Chap. 4.) Therefore all this proves that time, space, and causality do not come to us through sight, touch, or indeed at all from without, but rather that they have an internal origin, one that is not empirical but intellectual. Again it follows from this that intuitive perception of the corporeal world is essentially an intellectual process, a work of the understanding, for which the sensation merely furnishes the opportunity and the data for application in the particular case.

I wish now to demonstrate the same thing with regard to the sense of sight. What is directly given is here limited to the sensation of the retina which, though admitting of great variety, can be reduced to the impression of brightness and darkness together with their intermediate degrees, and to the impression of colours proper. This sensation is entirely subjective, in other words, exists only within the organism and beneath the skin. Moreover, without the understanding we should become conscious of those gradations only as particular and varied modifications of the sensation in our eye, and these would bear no resemblance to the shape, position, proximity, or distance of things

84

outside us. For in the case of vision the *sensation* supplies nothing more than a varied affection of the retina, exactly like the spectacle of a painter's palette with many different splashes of colour. And nothing more than this would be left in our consciousness if suddenly we were deprived entirely of our understanding, say by paralysis of the brain at a moment when we were contemplating a fine and extensive landscape, although the sensation might be left unchanged. For this was the raw material from which our understanding had just previously created that intuitive perception.

From such limited material as brightness, darkness and colour, the understanding is now able to produce, through its simple function of referring the effect to a cause and with the aid of the intuitive form of space given to it, the visible world that is inexhaustibly rich in its many different forms. All this first depends on the assistance that is here given by the sensation itself. The nature of this is that first the retina as a surface admits of a juxtaposition of impressions; secondly, that light always acts in straight lines, and even in the eye itself its refraction is rectilinear; and finally, that the retina possesses the faculty of immediately feeling from which direction the light impinges on it, its ability so to do being explained possibly from the fact that the ray of light penetrates beneath its surface. But the result of this is that the mere impression already indicates the direction of its cause, and thus points directly to the locality of the object that is emitting or reflecting the light. The transition to this object as cause naturally presupposes a knowledge both of the causal relation and of

85

The intellect creates intuitive perception

the laws of space. Such knowledge, however, is just the equipment of the *intellect* which again has to create here intuitive perception from the mere sensation. We will now consider in more detail the way in which it does this.

The first thing it does is again to set right the impression of the object which appears reversed and upside down on the retina. We know that this inversion is brought about in the following way. As each point of the visible object sends out its rays in straight lines in all directions, the rays from the upper end of the object cross those from the lower in the narrow aperture of the pupil. Thus the former impinge on the bottom, the latter on the top, and likewise those coming from the left impinge on the right, and vice versa. The refracting apparatus in the eye, the *humor aqueus, lens et corpus vitreum*, merely serves to concentrate the rays of light from the object, so that they will be accommodated in the small space of the retina. Now if vision consisted in mere sensation, we should perceive the impression of the object reversed and upside down because we receive it in this way. But then we should also perceive it as something existing within our eye, for we should stop short at the sensation. Actually, however, the understanding steps in at once with its causal law, refers the experienced effect to its cause, and, as from the sensation it has the datum of the direction in which the ray of light impinged on the retina, it pursues this backwards to the cause on both lines. Consequently the crossing is now gone through in the reverse direction, whereby the cause presents itself, upright and outside, as an object in space, namely in the position in which it sends out the rays, not in that in which they reach the retina. (See Fig. 1.) The purely intellectual nature of

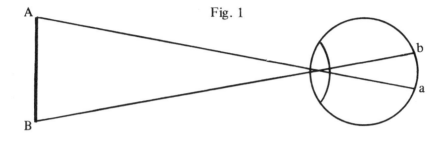

Fig. 1

the process, to the exclusion of all other explanations, especially the physiological, may be confirmed also by the fact that, if we put our heads between our legs or lie head downwards on a steep slope, we nevertheless see things not upside down and reversed, but quite in order, although that part of the retina, usually affected by the lower part of things, is now affected by the upper; in fact everything is reversed, but not the understanding.

The second thing the understanding does in converting the sensation into intuitive perception is to make one single perception out of a doubly experienced sensation; for by itself and also in a somewhat different direction each eye receives an impression of the object, yet such object presents itself as a single one, and this can occur only in the understanding. The following is the process by which this is brought about. Our eyes are parallel only when we look at an object that is more than two hundred feet away; otherwise both are directed to the object we are looking at, whereby they converge, and the two lines, one from each eye to the exactly fixed point of the object, there form an *angle* called the *optical angle*, the lines themselves being called the *axes of the eye*. In the case of an object right in front of us, these lines impinge on the very centre of each retina, and so on two *points exactly corresponding* to each other in each eye. Always looking merely for the *cause* of everything, the understanding at once recognizes that, although the impression is double here, this nevertheless comes from only *one* point outside. Hence only *one* cause forms the basis of this impression, and accordingly such cause now presents itself as merely a single object. For everything perceived by us is perceived as *cause*, as the cause of an effect experienced by us, consequently *in the understanding*. As, however, we perceive not merely one point, but a considerable surface of the object with both eyes, and yet perceive only a single object, the given explanation must be carried still further. Those points of the object, which lie to one side of the vertex of the optical angle, no longer cast their rays straight into the centre of each retina, but to one side thereof, yet in both eyes to the same side, for instance, to the left side of each retina. Therefore the points on which these rays there impinge are, just like the centre points, those *symmetrically correspond-ing to each other*; or they are *homonymous points*. The understanding soon learns to know these, and accordingly extends to *them* also the above-mentioned rule of its causal intuitive perception. Consequently, it refers not only the light rays impinging on the centre of each retina, but also those that fall on the other *symmetrically corresponding*

points of the two retinas, to one and the same point in the
object emitting the rays. Therefore all these points and
hence the whole object are perceived by it only *singly*. Now
here it should be carefully noted that it is not the outer side
of one retina that corresponds the outer side of the other,
and the inner to the inner, but the right side of the right
retina which corresponds to the right side of the other, and
so forth. Therefore the matter must be conceived in the
geometrical, and not in the physiological, sense. Clear and
numerous figures illustrating this process and all the
phenomena connected therewith are found in Robert
Smith's *Optics*, and to some extent also in Kastner's
German translation of 1755. In Figure 2 I have given only

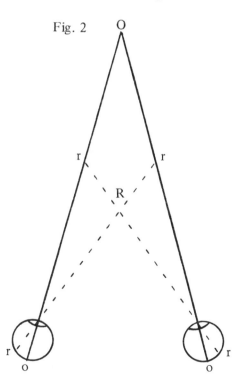

Fig. 2

one that really represents a special case to be mentioned later on; yet it can serve to illustrate the whole thing if we entirely disregard the point R. According to this, we always turn both eyes symmetrically to the object in order to apprehend with the symmetrically corresponding points on the two retinas the rays that emanate from the same points. When we move our eyes sideways, upwards, downwards, and in all directions, the point of the object which previously impinged on the centre of each retina now strikes a different spot each time, but invariably in both eyes a homonymous spot corresponding to that in the other eye. If we examine an object (*perlustrare*), we allow our eyes to move over it in order to bring each point of it successively in contact with the centre of the retina which sees most distinctly; thus we feel the object with our eyes. It is clear from this that single vision with two eyes is at bottom the same as touching and feeling a body with ten fingers, each of which receives a different impression, moreover from a different direction. But the understanding recognizes all these impressions as originating from one body whose shape and size it accordingly apprehends and constructs in space. This is why it is possible for a blind man to be a sculptor, as was the case with the famous Joseph Kleinhanns who died in the Tyrol in 1853, and had been a sculptor since he was five.[*] For intuitive perception takes place always through the understanding, no matter from what sense it obtains the data.

Now when I touch a sphere with fingers crossed, I at once imagine I am touching two spheres because my understanding, reverting to the cause and constructing this according to the laws of space, assumes the natural position of the fingers, and is bound to attribute to two different spheres two spherical surfaces that are simultaneously touched by the outer sides of the index and middle fingers. In the same way, an object will appear to me double, if my eyes, instead of converging symmetrically and closing the optical angle at *one* point on the object, now see it each at a different angle, in other words, if I squint. For now the symmetrically corresponding points on the two retinas are no longer impinged on by the rays emanating from *one* point of the object, points with which my understanding has grown familiar through constant experience. On the contrary, quite different points are impinged on, and therefore those which with a symmetrical position of the eyes could be affected only by different bodies. Therefore I now see *two* objects just because intuitive perception takes place through the understanding and in the understanding. The same thing occurs without squinting when I see before me two objects at unequal distances, and look steadily at the more distant, thereby closing at it the optical angle. For now the rays that emanate from the nearer object will impinge on the two retinas at points which do not correspond symmetrically. Therefore my understanding will attribute them to two objects, that is to say, I shall see the nearer object double. (See Fig. 2.) On the other hand, if I complete the optical angle at the nearer object by looking steadily at it, then for the same reason the more distant object will appear double. To test this, we can hold a pencil two feet from the eyes, and look alternately at the pencil and at the more distant object behind it.

But best of all, the reverse experiment can be made so that, with two actual objects right in front of and close to us and with our eyes open, we nevertheless see only *one*. This is the most striking proof that intuitive perception is certainly not to be found in the sensation, but takes place through an act of the understanding. Take two cardboard tubes about eight inches in length and one and a half in diameter, fix them absolutely parallel to each other similar to those of a binocular telescope, and place a coin at the end of each tube. If we now put the other ends of the tubes to our eyes and look through them, we shall perceive only *one* coin surrounded by *one* tube. Being forced by the tubes into an absolutely parallel position, the two eyes are impinged on by the two coins at the exact centre of each retina and quite symmetrically at the points which surround each centre and therefore symmetrically correspond to each other. And so, taking for granted the otherwise usual, indeed necessary, convergent position of the axes of the eyes in the case of near objects, the understanding assumes a single object as the cause of the reflected light; in other words, we see only one object, so direct is the causal apprehension of the understanding.

Here we have no room for refuting one by one the attempts at a physiological explanation of single vision, but their fallacy is clear from the following considerations. (1) If the thing depended on an organic connexion, the mutually corresponding spots on the two retinas, on which single vision is shown to depend, would inevitably be homonymous in the *organic* sense; but, as already stated, they are so only in the *geometrical*. For organically the two inner and the two outer corners of the eye correspond to each other, and everything else in the same way. On the other hand, for the purpose of single vision, the right side of the right retina corresponds to the right side of the left retina, and so on, as is irrefutably clear from the above phenomena. Just because the thing is intellectual, only the most intelligent animals, the higher mammals, and birds of prey, especially owls, have their eyes so placed as to enable them to direct both axes of the eyes on to the one point. (2) The hypothesis of a confluence or partial intersection of the optic nerves prior to their entry into the brain, which was first advanced by Newton (*Optics*, Query 15), is false, since double vision through squinting would then be impossible. Moreover, Vesalius and Caesalpinus have mentioned anatomical instances in which absolutely no intermingling, indeed no contact, of the optic nerves took place, yet the subjects had a single vision of things. Finally, the following argues against that intermingling of impression. If we shut the right eye and look at the sun with the left, then only in the left eye, never in the right, shall we have the subsequently lasting image of the sun's glare, or vice versa.

The third factor whereby the understanding converts sensation into intuitive perception consists in the construction of bodies from mere surfaces previously obtained, and hence in the addition of the third dimension. This it does by causally estimating the extension of bodies in that dimension, in space that is known to it a priori, according to the degree of their impression on the eye, and to the gradations of light and shade. Thus whereas objects fill space in all three dimensions, they can act on the eye only with two; in consequence of the nature of the organ, the sensation in vision is merely planimetric, not stereometric. Everything stereometric in intuitive perception is first added by the understanding; and that faculty's only data for this are the direction whence the eye receives the impression, the limits of this, and the different degrees of brightness and darkness. All these data point directly to their causes, and accordingly we know whether, for example, we have before us a disc or a ball. Moreover, this operation of the understanding, like those others, is carried out so directly and rapidly that we are conscious of nothing but the result. For this very reason drawing in perspective is so difficult a problem, to be solved only by mathematical principles; and it must first be learnt, although it has nothing to do but to represent the sensation of vision, as given to this third operation of the understanding. Thus it represents the sensation of vision in its merely planimetric extension, and to the given *two* dimensions of this together with the aforesaid data therein the understanding at once adds the third when looking at the drawing as well as at reality. Such a drawing is therefore a kind of writing which, like printed type, everyone can read but few can write. This is because our perceiving intellect apprehends the effect simply in order to construct therefrom the cause, but at once entirely disregards the former when it has arrived at the latter. Thus, for instance, we instantly recognize a chair in every possible position, but to draw it in any position is the business of that art which abstracts from this third operation of the understanding in order to present simply the data for the spectator himself to complete. As I have said, this is primarily the art of drawing in perspective, but it is also that of painting in the widest sense. The picture furnishes lines drawn in accordance with the rules of perspective, bright and dark parts in accordance with the effect of light and shade, finally patches of colour that are learnt from experience as to quality and intensity. The spectator reads all this from the picture by attributing to similar effects their accustomed causes. The painter's art consists in knowing how to retain consciously the data of visual sensation as they are *prior* to this third operation of the understanding. On the other hand, as soon as we others have made the aforesaid use of them, we cast them aside without taking them into our memory. We shall become even better acquainted with this third operation of the understanding if we now pass to a fourth which, through being intimately associated with the third, also makes it clear.

This fourth operation of the understanding consists in our recognizing the distance of objects in front of us; but this is precisely the third dimension about which we have just spoken. As we have said, visual sensation gives us the *direction* in which objects lie, but not their *distance* and hence not their *place*. Distance must therefore be brought out first by the *understanding*, and so it must result from merely *causal* determinations. Now the most important of these is the *visual angle* subtended by the object; yet this is quite ambiguous and by itself alone cannot decide anything. It is like a word of two meanings; only from the context can we infer what is meant. For with the same visual angle an object may be small and near or large and distant. Only when its size is already known to us in another way are we able to know its distance from the visual angle, just as conversely when its distance is given to us in another way, we can ascertain its size. Linear perspective rests on a diminution of the visual angle in consequence of an increase in the distance, and here its principles can be readily deduced. Thus since our power of vision reaches equally in all directions, we really see everything as a hollow sphere in whose centre is our eye. Now in the first place, this sphere has an infinite number of intersecting circles in all directions, and the angles whose size is given by the parts or divisions of those circles are the possible visual angles. In the second place, this sphere becomes larger or smaller according as we assume its radius to be longer or shorter. Therefore we can also imagine it as consisting of an infinite number of concentric, transparent, hollow spheres. As all radii diverge, these concentric hollow spheres are the greater the more distant they are from us, and the degrees of their circles of intersection increase with them, and so the true size of the objects occupying these degrees also increases. Therefore these objects are greater or smaller according as they occupy the same portion (e.g., 10 degrees) of a larger or smaller hollow sphere, whereas their visual angles in both cases remains the same; thus we are left in suspense whether the ten degrees belong to a sphere of two miles or of ten feet in diameter which is occupied by their object. Conversely, if the size of this object has been ascertained, the number of degrees occupied by it will diminish in proportion as the hollow sphere to which we shift it is more distant and therefore larger; and so all its outlines will contract in similar proportion. From this we have the fundamental rule of all perspective; for, as objects and the intervals between them must diminish in constant proportion to their distance from us, whereby all their outlines contract, the result will be that, with increasing distance, everything above us descends, everything below us ascends, and all things at the sides are drawn closer together. Insofar as we have before us an uninterrupted succession of visibly connected objects, we are certainly able to judge distance from this gradual convergence of all lines and hence from linear perspective. Yet we cannot do this from the mere visual angle by itself, but the understanding must always summon to its aid another datum which acts, so to speak, as a commentary to the visual angle, since it indicates more definitely the share that distance has in that angle. Now there are essentially four such data, and I shall state them more specifically. By virtue thereof it happens that, even where I lack linear perspective in most cases, I at once estimate correctly the size of a person, although when standing a hundred feet from me he appears to subtend a visual angle twenty-four times smaller than he would if he stood two feet from me. All this proves once more that intuitive perception is the business of the intellect and not merely of the senses. The following is a special and interesting proof of the basis of linear perspective, as also of the intellectual nature of intuitive perception generally. If as a result of looking at a coloured object of definite outline, e.g., a red cross, I receive in my eye its physiological coloured after-image and thus a green cross, then this will appear to me the greater, the more distant the surface onto which I project it, and vice versa. For the after-image itself occupies a definite and unalterable part of my retina, the spot first affected by the red cross; and so, by being projected outwards, that is to say, by being apprehended as the effect of an external object, the after-image forms a visual angle that is given once for all, say of two degrees. Now if in this case (where all commentary to the visual angle is wanting) I shift that angle to a distant surface with which I inevitably identify it as belonging to the effect of that surface, then the two degrees are of a distant and therefore very large sphere that is occupied by the after-image, and consequently the cross is large. If, on the other hand, I project the after-image on to a near object, it fills two degrees of a smaller sphere, and is therefore small. In both cases the intuitive perception proves to be perfectly objective, precisely like that of an external object, and as it proceeds from a wholly subjective ground (from the after-image stimulated in quite a different way), it thus illustrates the intellectual nature of all objective intuitive perception. This fact (which I distinctly recall in detail, having first observed it in 1815) is discussed in the *Comptes Rendus* of 2 August 1858 in an article by M. Séguin. He serves it up here as a new discovery, and gives all sorts of erroneous and absurd explanations. *Messieurs les illustres confrères* lose no opportunity in heaping experiments on experiments, and the more complicated they are, the better. *Expérience* alone is their watchword; but very rarely indeed do we meet with a little sound and genuine reflection on the observed phenomena; *expérience, expérience*! and stuff and nonsense as well.

98

Of the above-mentioned subsidiary data that furnish the commentary to the given visual angle, we first have the *mutationes oculi internae*[20] by means whereof the eye accommodates its optical refractory apparatus to various distances by increasing or diminishing refraction. But it has never yet been settled what is the physiological nature of these changes. They have been sought in the increase of convexity first of the *cornea* and then of the *lens*. However, the more probable theory seems to be the most recent, expressed in essence by Kepler, according to which the lens moves backwards in distant vision and forwards in near, and is thus rendered more convex through lateral pressure; and so the process would be wholly analogous to the mechanism of a pair of opera glasses. This theory is discussed in detail by A. Hueck in his *Die Bewegung der Krystallinse*, 1841. At any rate we have a certain sensation of these internal changes in the eye, although we do not clearly perceive them, and we use them directly for estimating distance. But as those changes enable vision to be perfectly clear only within a range of from seven inches to sixteen feet, the aforesaid datum is applicable for the understanding only within that distance.

On the other hand, beyond this the second datum can be applied, namely the *optical angle* which is formed by the two axes of the eyes and was explained in connexion with single vision. This angle obviously becomes smaller, the farther the object is from us, and vice versa. This different adjustment of the eyes to each other is not without a certain slight sensation, but we are conscious of it only insofar as the understanding uses it as a datum in the intuitive judgement of distance. Moreover, this datum enables us to know not merely the distance, but also the precise *position* of the object, by means of the parallax of the eyes. This consists in each eye seeing the object in a somewhat different direction so that when we close one eye the object seems to move. Consequently, if we have one eye shut, we shall not find it easy to snuff a candle, because this datum is now wanting. But as soon as the object is at a distance of two hundred feet or more, the direction of the eyes becomes parallel and hence the optical angle disappears entirely. Therefore this datum holds good only within the aforesaid distance.

Beyond this, *atmospheric perspective* comes to the aid of the understanding and announces to it a greater distance through the increasing dimness of all colours, the appearance of physical blue in front of all dark objects (according to Goethe's perfectly true and correct colour theory), and the growing indistinctness of the contours. On account of the great transparency of the atmosphere, this datum is extremely feeble in Italy; and so in that country it easily misleads us. For example, Tivoli appears to be very near when seen from Frascati. On the other hand, all objects appear larger in a haze which is an abnormal enhancement of this datum, because the understanding assumes them to be more distant.

Finally, we are still left with the estimation of distance by means of the size (known to us intuitively) of intervening objects, such as fields, rivers, woods and so on. It is applicable only where there is an uninterrupted connexion and thus only to terrestrial, and not to celestial, objects. In general we are more experienced in using it horizontally than vertically; thus a ball on top of a tower two hundred feet high appears to be much smaller than when it lies on the ground two hundred feet from us, since here we estimate the distance more accurately. Whenever we come across people in such a way that the ground between us and them remains for the most part concealed, they seem to us to be surprisingly small.

Our intuitively perceiving understanding regards everything in a horizontal direction as more distant and consequently as larger than in a vertical. This is attributable partly to that last method of estimation, insofar as it is applicable only to terrestrial objects and in a horizontal direction; partly to estimation by atmospheric perspective to be found in the same case. This is why the moon appears so very much larger at the horizon than at its southing, whereas its accurately measured visual angle, and thus the image it projects on the eye, are certainly not greater. In the same way, the celestial vault appears flattened, in other words, to be of greater extension horizontally than vertically. Both phenomena are therefore purely intellectual or cerebral and not optical or sensuous. The objection that, even at its zenith, the moon is sometimes obscured and yet does not seem larger, can be met by saying that it also does not appear red, since the cloudiness occurs through a greater density of haze and mist and is therefore of a nature different from that produced by atmospheric perspective. It can also be refuted by the fact that, as I have said, we apply this estimation only horizontally and not in a perpendicular direction; moreover, in this case other correctives occur.

Saussure is reported to have seen so large a moon, when it rose over Mont Blanc, that he did not recognize it and fainted with terror.

On the other hand, the action of the telescope and of the magnifying glass is due to the isolated estimation according to the visual angle alone, thus to size through distance and to distance through size; for here the other four supplementary means of estimation are excluded. The telescope actually magnifies, but appears merely to bring objects nearer because their size is known to us empirically, and we now explain the apparent increase of their size from a shorter distance. Thus a house seen through the telescope appears to be not ten times larger, but ten times nearer. The magnifying glass, on the other hand, does not really magnify, but merely enables us to bring the object to our eyes nearer than would otherwise be possible; and it appears only as large as it would appear at such a short distance, even without the magnifying glass. Thus too little convexity of the *lens* and *cornea* does not permit us to see clearly at a distance of less than eight to ten inches. If, however, the refraction is now increased by the convexity of the magnifying glass instead of by that of the *cornea* and *lens*, we still obtain a clear image even at a distance of only half an inch from the eye. The object, seen at such close proximity and in a size corresponding thereto, is shifted by our understanding to the natural distance of clear vision and thus to a distance of eight to ten inches from the eye. Our understanding now estimates the size of the object according to this distance and to the given visual angle.

I have discussed at great length all these details

no understanding in taste
smell hearing

concerning vision in order to show clearly and irrefutably that the *understanding* is predominantly active therein. By conceiving every change as an *effect* and referring this to its cause the understanding brings about the cerebral phenomenon of the objective world on the basis of the fundamental a priori intuitions of space and time, and for this purpose sensation supplies it with only a few data. In fact the understanding carries out this business solely through its own form, the law of causality, and thus quite directly and intuitively, without the assistance of reflection, i.e., of abstract knowledge by means of concepts and words. These are the material of *secondary* knowledge, i.e., of *thought*, of the faculty of *reason* (*Vernunft*).

Knowledge of the understanding is independent of the reasoning faculty and its assistance. This is clear from the fact that, if at any time the understanding attributes to given effects a wrong cause, and consequently directly perceives that cause whereby *illusion* arises, the reasoning faculty may still know correctly *in abstracto* the true state of affairs, but yet cannot come to the aid of the understanding with such abstract knowledge; on the contrary, the illusion persists fixed and unmoved, regardless of that better abstract knowledge. The above-mentioned phenomena of double vision and double touch in consequence of the abnormal position of the organs of sense are an illustration of this kind; likewise the moon that appears to be greater at the horizon; the image formed at the focus of a concave mirror and floating in space exactly like a solid body; the painted relievo regarded as something real; the motion of the shore or of the bridge on which we are

X K Jud of Reason because of Decision

103

standing while a ship is sailing under it; high mountains that appear to be very much nearer than they are owing to a want of atmospheric perspective, this being the result of the purity of the air round their high peaks. In these and a hundred similar instances the understanding assumes the usual cause with which it is familiar. It therefore perceives this at once, although our reasoning faculty has discovered the correct state of affairs in different ways. The understanding, however, is inaccessible to the teaching of reason, since in its knowledge it precedes reason and so cannot be reached by that faculty. Thus *illusion*, i.e., deception of the understanding, persists unmoved, although *error*, i.e., deception of the faculty of reason, is prevented. What is correctly known by the *understanding* is *reality*; what is correctly known by the *faculty of reason* is *truth*, i.e., a judgement having a ground or reason (*Grund*). To reality is opposed *illusion* (what is falsely perceived); to truth is opposed *error* (what is falsely conceived).

Although the purely formal part of empirical intuitive perception and hence the law of causality together with space and time are contained a priori in the intellect, the application of this law to empirical data is not given to it simultaneously; on the contrary, it reaches this only through practice and experience. This is why new-born infants, who certainly receive impressions of light and colour, do not yet apprehend and really see objects. On the contrary, throughout the first weeks they are under a stupor that passes off when their understanding begins to exercise its function on the data of the senses, in particular of touch and sight, whereby the objective world gradually enters their consciousness. This dawning consciousness is clearly recognizable from the growing intelligence of their gaze and from a certain purpose and intention in their movements, especially when for the first time they show by a friendly smile that they recognize those who look after them. We can also watch them experimenting for a long time with sight and touch in order to complete their apprehension of objects under different illumination, in different directions, and at different distances. Thus we see them pursue a silent but serious study until they have learnt all the above-mentioned intellectual operations of vision. Nevertheless this schooling can be much more clearly verified in the case of those who are born blind and have undergone an operation late in life; for they are able to give an account of their observations. Cheselden's blind man became famous (the original account of him appears in Vol. 35 of the *Philosophical Transactions*), and there have since been repeated instances of this. It is always confirmed that those obtaining the use of their eyes late in life certainly see light, colours, and outlines immediately after the operation, but yet have no objective perception of things; for their understanding must first learn to apply its causal law to the data that are new to it, and to the changes thereof. When Cheselden's blind man for the first time saw his room with its different objects, he did not distinguish anything, but had only a general impression as of a totality consisting of a single piece which he took to be a smooth surface of different colours. It never occurred to him to recognize separate things lying behind one another at different distances. With the blind who have thus obtained their sight

the sense of touch to which things are already familiar must
first make them acquainted with the sense of vision, must
present and introduce them, so to speak. To begin with,
such people have absolutely no capacity for judging
distances, but grasp at everything. When one such person
saw his house from outside, he could not believe how all
the large rooms could exist in so small a thing. Another was
highly delighted when he made the discovery some weeks
after his operation that the copper engravings on the wall
represented all kinds of objects. In the *Morgenblatt* of 23
October 1817 there is an account of one born blind who
obtained his sight at the age of seventeen. He first had to
learn intelligent intuitive perception; when he saw an object
previously known to him through touch he did not again
recognize it; and thus he mistook goats for human beings,
and so on. The sense of touch first of all had to make that
of sight acquainted with every single object. In the same
way he had absolutely no capacity for judging the distance
of objects seen by him, but reached out for everything. In
his book: *The Eye: A Treatise on the Art of preserving this
Organ in healthy Condition, and of improving the Sight*
(London: Churchill, 1839) Franz says on pages 34-36: "A
definite idea of distance, as well as of form and size, is only
obtained by sight and touch, and by reflecting on the
impressions made on both senses; but for this purpose we
must take into account the muscular motion and voluntary
locomotion of the individual." Caspar Hausar,[21] in a
detailed account of his own experience in this respect,
states that upon his first liberation from confinement,
whenever he looked through the window upon external

objects, such as the street, garden, etc., it appeared to him as if there were a shutter quite close to his eye, and covered with confused colours of all kinds, in which he could recognize or distinguish nothing singly. He says farther that he did not convince himself till after some time during his walks out of doors, that what had first appeared to him as a shutter of various colours, as well as many objects, were in reality very different things; and that at length the shutter disappeared, and he saw and recognized all things in their just proportions. Persons born blind who obtain their sight by an operation in later years only, sometimes imagine that all objects touch their eyes, and lie so near to them that they are afraid of stumbling against them; sometimes they leap towards the moon, supposing that they can lay hold of it; at other times they run after the clouds moving along the sky, in order to catch them, or commit other such extravagancies . . . . Since ideas are gained by reflection upon sensation, it is further necessary in all cases, in order that an accurate idea of objects may be formed from the sense of sight, that the powers of the mind should be unimpaired, and undisturbed in their exercise. A proof of this is afforded in the instance related by Haslam[2] of a boy who had no defect of sight, but was weak in understanding, and who in his seventh year was unable to estimate the distances of objects, especially as to height; he would extend his hand frequently towards a nail on the ceiling, or towards the moon, to catch it. It is therefore the judgement which corrects and makes clear this idea, or perception of visible objects."

The intellectual nature of intuitive perception, here

discussed is confirmed physiologically by Flourens: *De la vie et de l'intelligence* (*Deuxième édition*; Paris: Garnier Freres, 1858). He says on page 49 under the heading: *Opposition entre les tubercles et les lobes cérébraux*: "We must make a great distinction between the senses and the understanding. The removal of a cerebral tubercle determines the loss of *sensation*, of the *sense* of sight; the retina becomes insensible, the iris becomes set. The removal of a cerebral lobe allows *sensation, sense, sensibility* of the retina and *mobility* of the iris to continue; it destroys simply *perception*. In the one case we are concerned with a *sensorial* fact, in the other with a *cerebral*; in the one case it is the loss of *sense*, in the other the loss of *perception*. The distinction of perceptions and sensations is nevertheless a great result, and its demonstration is obvious. There are two means of causing loss of vision through the brain: (1) through the tubercles, that is the loss of sense, of sensation; (2) through the lobes, that is the loss of perception, of intelligence. Accordingly, sensibility is not intelligence or understanding, thinking is not feeling; and thus an entire philosophy is upset. Therefore the mental conception is not sensation; and here we have a new proof of the radical defect of this philosophy." Further on page 77 under the heading: *Séparation de la Sensibilité et de la Perception*: "One of my experiments shows that we must clearly distinguish between *sensibility* and *perception*. If we remove an animal's *brain in the real sense* (the *lobes* or *cerebral hemispheres*), the animal loses its sight. But with regard to the eye nothing has altered; objects continue to be projected on the retina; the *iris* remains contractile, and

reason & understanding oppose each other in sight Con. I.P.

the *optic nerve* perfectly sensitive and responsive. And yet the animal no longer sees; there is no longer any *vision*, although everything appertaining to *sensation* continues to exist; there is no longer any *vision* because there is no longer any *perception*. Consequently *perceiving* and not *feeling* is the first element of the *intelligence* or *understanding*. *Perception* is the business of the *intelligence*, for it is lost along with *intelligence* and by the removal of the same organ, namely the *lobes* or *cerebral hemispheres. Sensibility* is not its business at all, since it continues to exist after the loss of *intelligence* and the removal of the *lobes* or *hemispheres*." [Tr.][23]

The famous verse of the philosopher Epicharmus proves that the ancients also understood in general the intellectual nature of intuitive perception:

"Only the mind can see and hear; everything else is deaf and blind." [Tr.][24] Plutarch quotes it *De sollertia animalium,* c. 3), and adds: "But sensation in our eyes and ears does not produce any perception in the absence of intelligence," [Tr.][25] and shortly before he says: "It is the theory of the natural philosopher Straton who shows that without intelligence it is quite impossible to perceive." [Tr.][26] But shortly afterwards he says: "Therefore all beings that perceive must also have intelligence, since only through intelligence are we able to perceive." [Tr.][27] A second verse of Epicharmus, quoted by Diogenes Laërtius (III, 16), might be related to this:

"Sagacity, O Eumaeus, does not belong to us alone, but every living being also has intellect." [Tr.][28]

Porphyry (*De abstinentia,* III, 21) also attempts to demonstrate in detail that all animals have understanding.

Now that this is so, follows necessarily from the intellectual nature of intuitive perception. All animals, even the lowest, must have understanding, that is to say, knowledge of the law of causality, although they may have it in very different degrees of keenness and clearness. At any rate they must always have as much as is necessary for intuitive perception with their senses; for sensation without understanding would be not merely a useless, but even a cruel, gift of nature. No one who himself has any intelligence will doubt its existence in the higher animals. But it is at times quite evident that their knowledge of causality is actually a priori, and has not resulted from the habit of seeing one thing follow another. A young puppy does not jump down from a table because he anticipates the effect. At my bedroom window large curtains were recently installed reaching down to the floor, the kind that are drawn apart from the centre when a cord is pulled. One morning I got up and pulled the cord for the first time and, to my astonishment, noticed that my very intelligent poodle stood there in amazement, looking up and to the side for the cause of the phenomenon. He was looking for the change which he knew a priori must have previously taken place. The same thing happened again the following morning. But the lowest animals, even water-polyps without separate organs of sense, have perception and therefore understanding, when, in order to reach brighter light, they wander on their aquatic plant from leaf to leaf, clinging thereto with their feelers.

Between this lowest understanding and that of man,

which we nevertheless clearly distinguish from his faculty of reason, the difference is only one of degree. All the intermediate gradations are filled by the series of animals, the highest members of which, such as the monkey, elephant, and dog, astonish us with their understanding. But the business of the understanding always and invariably consists in the immediate apprehension of causal relations, first, as I have shown, between our own and other bodies, the result of this being objective intuitive perception; then between these objectively perceived bodies among themselves where, as we saw in the previous paragraph, the causality-relation now appears in three different forms, as cause, stimulus, and motive. All movement in the world then takes place according to these three, and is understood by the understanding alone. Now if of these three it is *causes* in the narrowest sense that the understanding investigates, it produces mechanics, astronomy, physics, chemistry, and invents machines for prosperity and perdition. However, in the last resort, an immediate intuitive apprehension of the causal connexion is invariably the basis of all its discoveries. For this is the sole form and function of the understanding, certainly not the complicated clockwork of the twelve Kantian categories whose invalidity I have shown. All understanding is an immediate, and therefore intuitive, apprehension of the causal connexion, although to be fixed it must be reduced at once to abstract concepts. Therefore calculating is not understanding and in itself does not afford a comprehension of things. Only on the path of intuitive perception do we get this through a correct knowledge of causality and the *geometrical* con-

111

struction of the sequence of events. Euler gave this better than anyone else because he had a thorough understanding of things. Calculation, on the other hand, is concerned with nothing but abstract concepts of quantities whose mutual relations are determined thereby. In this way we never arrive at the slightest comprehension of a physical process. For such a comprehension requires the *intuitive* apprehension of spatial relations by means of which causes operate. Calculation determines how many and how large and is therefore indispensable in *practical* affairs. It can even be said that *where calculating begins, understanding ends*; for whoever is occupied with numbers is, while calculating, a complete stranger to the causal connexion and to geometrical construction of the physical sequence of events; he is engrossed in purely abstract numerical concepts. But the result never states more than *how much*; never *what*. Therefore *l'expérience et le calcul*, those watchwords of French physicists, are certainly not enough. On the other hand, if *stimuli* are the guiding line of the understanding, it will bring about the physiology of plants and animals, therapy, and toxicology. Finally, if the understanding has turned to *motivation*, it will use this, on the one hand, merely theoretically as a guide for the advancement of morality, jurisprudence, history, politics, and even of dramatic and epic poetry; on the other hand, it will make practical use of motivation either to train animals, or even to make the human race dance to its tune, after it has succeeded in discovering which string is pulled, so that each puppet moves at its pleasure. Now with regard to the function here at work, it is all the same whether the understanding takes such ingenious advantage of the weight of bodies by means of mechanics for machines that their effect serves its purpose by stepping in at just the right moment; or whether it brings into play for its own ends the collective or individual propensities of men. Now in this practical application the understanding is called prudence or judiciousness, and, when accompanied by the deception of others, it is called cunning. When its aims are insignificant, it is craftiness; and when it is related to the injury of others, it is called roguery or knavery. On the other hand, in its merely theoretical use, it is simply called *understanding*; in its higher degrees it is called acumen, insight, sagacity, discernment, penetration, whereas a want of understanding is called dullness, stupidity, silliness, and so on. These extremely different degrees of sharpness are inborn and cannot be acquired; although practice and knowledge of the material are everywhere needed for correct application, as indeed we have seen even in the first use of the understanding and thus in empirical intuitive perception. Every simpleton has the faculty of reason; give him the premisses, and he will draw the conclusion. But the understanding supplies *primary*, and therefore intuitive, cf. p. knowledge, and here we find the differences. Accordingly, 104 the pith of every great discovery as well as of every world plan of historical importance is the product of a propitious moment when, through favourable outer and inner circumstances, complicated causal series or concealed causes of phenomena seen already a thousand times, or obscure paths never previously followed, suddenly reveal themselves to the understanding.

From the previous explanations of what happens when we touch and see, it has been incontestably shown that empirical intuitive perception is essentially the work of the *understanding.* For this perception the senses furnish the understanding merely with material which is in their sensations and is generally poor and scanty. Thus the *understanding* is the artist forming the work, whereas the *senses* are merely the assistants who hand up the materials. But its method here consists throughout in passing from given effects to their causes which thus present themselves first as objects in space. For this purpose the law of causality is presupposed, and this is precisely why it must have been supplied by the understanding itself, for it could never have come to the understanding from without. Indeed if this law is the first condition of all empirical intuitive perception, and yet such perception is the form in which all external experience appears, how could such a law be first drawn from experience whose essential presupposition is that law itself? Just because it cannot possibly do this, and because Locke's philosophy had put an end to all *a priority,* Hume denied the entire reality of the concept of causality. In this connexion he stated (in the seventh of his *Essays on Human Understanding*) two false hypotheses which have again been advanced in our day; one that the effect of the will on the limbs of the body, the other that the resistance offered by bodies when we press them, is the origin and prototype of the concept of causality. Hume refutes both in his own way and according to his own association of ideas. But I say that between the act of will and the bodily action there is no causal connexion

114

whatever; on the contrary, the two are directly one and the same thing perceived in a double way, namely in self-consciousness or the inner sense as an act of will, and simultaneously in external spatial brain-perception, as bodily action. (Cf. *World as Will and Representation*, Vol. II, Chap. 4) The second hypothesis is false because, as I have already shown in detail, a mere sensation of touch certainly does not give us any objective intuitive perception, let alone the concept of causality. This concept can never arise merely from the feeling of an impeded bodily exertion; indeed such an impediment often occurs without an external cause; and secondly because our pressing against an external object must have a motive, and already presupposes an intuitive perception of the object, but such perception presupposes knowledge of causality. The concept of causality is independent of all experience; this could be thoroughly demonstrated only by showing, as I have, that all experience and its whole possibility are dependent on this concept. In § 23 I shall show that Kant's proof, propounded with the same intention, is false.

This is also the place for drawing attention to the fact that Kant either did not clearly see that empirical intuitive perception is brought about by the law of causality which is known to us prior to all experience, or intentionally refrained from mentioning it, because it did not suit his purpose. In the *Critique of Pure Reason* the relation between causality and intuitive perception is not mentioned in the Doctrine of Elements, but at a place where on would not expect to find it, namely in the chapter on the Paralogisms of Pure Reason. Moreover, it is dealt with in the Critique of the Fourth Paralogism of Transcendental Psychology, and only in the first edition, p. 367 *et sqq.* The fact that this place was assigned to that discussion shows us that, when considering this relation, he always had in view only the transition from the phenomenon to the thing-in-itself, not the origin of intuitive perception itself. Accordingly, he says there that the existence of an actual object outside us is not given directly in perception, but can be added in thought as the external cause thereof, and so can be inferred. But whoever does this is in his opinion a transcendental realist, and therefore on the wrong path. For by "external object" Kant here means the thing-in-itself. The transcendental idealist, on the other hand, stops short at the perception of something empirically real, in other words, of something existing outside us in space, without having to infer a cause of perception in order to give it reality. Thus, according to Kant, *perception* is something quite direct and brought about entirely without the assistance of the causal nexus and thus of the understanding; he simply identifies perception with sensation. This is confirmed by the passage on page 371: "With reference to the reality of external objects, there is as little need for me to trust to inference," and so on, and also by the passage on page 372: "Indeed it can be admitted that" and so on. It is perfectly clear from these passages that, according to Kant, the *perception* of external things in space precedes all application of the causal law, that therefore the causal law does not enter into perception as an element and condition thereof; for him mere sensation is at once perception. Only insofar as we ask what may exist outside us, understood in the *transcendental* sense, and so when we ask about the thing-in-itself, is causality mentioned in connexion with perception. Moreover, Kant admits the existence and possibility of the causal law only in reflection and hence in the abstract distinct knowledge of concepts. He therefore has no conception that the application of the causal law *precedes all reflection*, and yet this is obviously the case, especially in empirical sensuous intuitive perception which would otherwise never take place; this I have irrefutably proved in the above analysis of intuitive perception. Kant therefore has to leave wholly unexplained the origin of empirical intuitive perception; with him it is a mere matter of the senses, given as it were by a miracle, and so is identical with sensation. I would very much like the attentive reader to look up the above-quoted passage of Kant in order to see clearly how very much more accurate is my conception of the whole sequence and process. In philosophical literature Kant's extremely erroneous view has prevailed ever since, because no one ventured to attack it, and here I found it necessary first to clear the ground in order to throw more light on the mechanism of our knowledge.

For the rest, the fundamental idealistic view advanced by Kant has lost absolutely nothing through my rectification; on the contrary, it has gained insofar as with me the demand of the causal law vanishes and is abolished in empirical intuitive perception as its product. Consequently, such demand cannot be extended to a wholly transcendent question about the thing-in-itself. Thus if we refer to my previous theory of empirical intuitive perception, we find

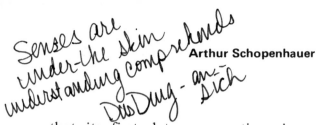

Senses are under the skin understanding comprehends Das Ding - an-sich

Arthur Schopenhauer

that its first datum, sensation, is something absolutely subjective, a process within the organism because it is beneath the skin. Locke has shown fully and thoroughly that these sensations of the organs of sense, even assuming their stimulation by external causes, cannot possibly have the slightest resemblance to the nature and quality of those causes, thus that sugar bears no resemblance to sweetness, or a rose to redness. But even that they must have an external cause at all, depends on a law whose origin lies demonstrably within us, within our brain. Consequently, this necessity is ultimately just as subjective as is the sensation itself. In fact *time*, this primary condition of the possibility of every *change* and so too of the change by virtue whereof the application of the concept of causality can first occur, and also *space*, which first renders possible the shifting outwards of a cause then presenting itself as object, are subjective forms of the intellect, as Kant has conclusively demonstrated. Accordingly, we find residing within ourselves all the elements of empirical intuitive perception and nothing in them that would reliably point to something absolutely different from us, to a thing-in-itself. But this is not all; with the concept of *matter* we think of what is still left of bodies when we divest them of their form and of all their specific qualities, a residue which, precisely on this account, must be one and the same in all bodies. But now those forms and qualities that are eliminated by us are nothing but the peculiar and specially determined *mode of operation* of bodies, and this precisely constitutes their difference. If, then, we disregard these forms and qualities, all that is left is *mere activity in*

118

general, pure acting as such, causality itself, objectively conceived, thus the reflection of our own understanding, the outwardly projected image of its sole function, and matter is throughout pure causality; its essence is action in general. (Cf. *World as Will and Representation*, Vol. I, Chap. 4, and Vol. II, Chap. 4.) This is why pure matter cannot be perceived but only conceived; it is something added in thought to every reality as the basis thereof. For pure causality, mere action, without a definite mode of action, cannot be given in intuitive perception, and so cannot occur in any experience. Matter is therefore only the objective correlative of the pure understanding; thus it is causality in general and nothing else, just as the understanding is immediate knowledge of cause and effect in general and nothing else. Now this again is precisely why the law of causality is not applicable to matter itself; in other words, matter cannot arise or pass away, but is and remains permanent. For all change and fluctuation of accidents (forms and qualities), i.e., all arising and passing away, occur only by virtue of causality, but matter is pure causality itself as such viewed objectively. Therefore it cannot exercise its own power on itself, just as the eye can see everything except itself. Moreover, as "substance" is identical with matter, we can say that *substance* is *action* viewed *in abstracto*; *accident* the particular mode of action, action *in concreto*. These, then, are the results to which true, i.e., transcendental, idealism leads. In my chief work I have shown that, on the path of the representation, we can never reach the thing-in-itself, i.e., that which exists generally outside the representation, but that for this

119

purpose we must pursue quite a different path leading through the heart of things and opening for us the citadel by treachery so to speak.

But it would be downright chicanery and nothing else, if the attempt were made to compare or even identify the honest and thorough analysis here given of empirical intuitive perception into its elements, such elements proving to be subjective, with Fichte's algebraical equations between the *ego* and *non-ego*; with that sophist's pseudo-demonstrations, requiring the cloak of incomprehensibility and even nonsense to deceive the reader; with explanations such as the *ego* spinning the *non-ego* out of itself; in short, with all the tomfoolery of scientific emptiness.[29] I protest against all association with this man Fichte just as Kant did publicly and expressly in an *ad hoc* notice in the *Jena'sche Litteratur-Zeitung*. (Kant: *Statement concerning Fichte's Doctrine of Science*, on the intelligence page of the *Jena'sche Litteratur-Zeitung*, 1799, No. 109.) Hegelians and like ignoramuses may continue to talk of a Kant-Fichtean philosophy; there is Kantian philosophy, and there is Fichtean humbug; this is and will always be the true state of affairs, in spite of all who extol the bad and belittle the good. For they are more numerous in the Fatherland than in any other country.

§ 22. On the Immediate Object

It is therefore the sensations of the body which give us the data for the very first application of the causal law, and it is from this very application that the intuitive perception of this class of objects arises. Consequently this class has its essence and existence only by virtue and in the exercise of the understanding's function that has thus ensued.

Now insofar as the organic body is the starting-point for the intuitive perception of all other objects and therefore helps to bring this about, I had called it in the first edition of this essay the *immediate object*; yet this expression can be applied only in a very figurative sense. For although the perception of the body's sensations is absolutely immediate, yet the body itself is by no means presented as object; on the contrary, everything so far still remains subjective, namely sensation. From this there certainly arises the intuitive perception of all other objects as the causes of such sensations, whereupon those causes present themselves as objects. The body itself, however, is different, for here it furnishes consciousness with mere sensations. Only *indirectly* is it known objectively and hence as object, since, like all other objects, it presents itself in the understanding or in the brain (which is the same thing) as the recognized cause of the subjectively given effect, and precisely in this way presents itself *objectively*. This can happen only by the body's parts acting each on its own senses, thus by the eye seeing the body, the hand touching it, and so on, and on these data

immediate object - starting point of for I.p

the brain or understanding spatially constructs it, like other objects, according to its shape and condition. Consequently, the immediate presence in our consciousness of representations of this class depends on the position assigned to them in the concatenation of causes and effects which links everything, relatively to the all-knowing subject's body for the time being.

§ 23. Arguments Against Kant's Proof of the A Priori Nature of the Concept of Causality

A principal object of the *Critique of Pure Reason* is to demonstrate the universal validity of the law of causality for all experience, its a priori nature, and, following therefrom, its restriction to the possibility of experience. I cannot, however, agree to the proof there given of the a priori nature of the principle. This proof is essentially as follows: "The synthesis of the manifold through the power of imagination—a synthesis that is necessary for all empirical knowledge—gives succession, but not yet a definite succession; that is to say, it leaves undetermined which of two perceived states comes first not only in my imagination but in the object. However, definite order of this succession, by which alone what is perceived becomes experience, in other words, justifies us in forming objectively valid judgements, first appears through the purely intellectual concept of cause and effect. Hence the principle of the

122

Kant criticisms

causal relation is the condition of the possibility of experience, and as such is given to us a priori." (See *Critique of Pure Reason,* 1st ed., p. 201; 5th ed., p. 246.)

According to this, the order of succession of changes in real objects is said to be recognized as objective first by means of their causality. Kant repeats and explains this assertion in the *Critique of Pure Reason,* especially in his "Second Analogy of Experience" (1st ed., p. 198; more fully in the 5th ed., p. 232). and then at the end of his "Third Analogy." I request all who wish to understand the following remarks to refer to these passages. In them he everywhere asserts that the *objectivity of the succession of representations,* which he declares to be their consistency and agreement with the succession of real objects, is known simply through the rule by which they follow one another, in other words, through the law of causality. He therefore asserts that through my mere apprehension, the objective relation between phenomena following one another remains quite undetermined, since I then apprehend merely the sequence of my representations, but the sequence in my apprehension does not entitle me to form a judgement of the sequence in the object, unless my judgement is supported by the law of causality; moreover, in my apprehension I could make the succession of perceptions proceed in quite the reverse order, there being nothing that determines them as objective. To illustrate this assertion, Kant mentions the case of a house whose parts he can consider in any order or succession he likes, thus from top to bottom and from bottom to top, where the determination of succession would be merely subjective, and not

Kant says real ob. have their objectivity first

Schopenhauer says the immediate object

based on an object, because it depends on his arbitrary choice. As a contrast to this, he quotes the perception of a ship sailing down a river which he first perceives up-stream and then successively more and more down-stream. He cannot change this perception of the succession in the positions of the ship. He therefore derives the subjective sequence of his apprehension here from the objective sequence in the phenomenon which he thus calls an *event*. On the other hand, I maintain that *the two cases are not different at all,* that both are events, the knowledge of which is objective, in other words, one of changes in real objects that are known as such by the subject. *Both are changes in the position of two bodies relatively to each other.* In the first case one of these bodies is the observer's own organism, and indeed only a part thereof, namely his eye, and the other is the house; with respect to the parts of the house, the position of the eye is successively changed. In the second case the ship alters its position relatively to the river, and so the change is between two bodies. Both are events; the only difference is that in the first case the change starts from the observer's own body whose sensations are naturally the starting-point of all his perceptions. Yet this body is nevertheless an object among objects, consequently is liable to the laws of this objective corporeal world. Insofar as he behaves as a purely knowing being, the movement of his body according to his will is for him merely an empirically perceived fact. The order of succession in the change could be reversed just as easily in the second case as in the first, if only the observer had the strength to pull the ship up-stream, just as he has to move his eye in the opposite direction. From the fact that the succession in the perceptions of the parts of the house depends on his own arbitrary choice, Kant tries to infer that this succession is not objective and not an event. But moving his eye from the roof to the basement is one event, and the opposite movement from basement to roof is another, just as is the sailing of the ship. Here there is absolutely no difference; in the same way, as regards their being events, there is no difference between my passing a squad of soldiers and their passing me; both are events. If from the shore I fix my eyes on a ship that is sailing quite close to where I am standing, it will soon appear to me that the shore and I are moving, and that the ship is standing still. Here, of course, I am mistaken as to the cause of the relative change of position, since I attribute the movement to a wrong object. But yet I objectively and correctly recognize the real succession of the positions of my body relative to the ship. Even in the case quoted by him, Kant could not have believed that there was any difference, had he borne in mind that his own body was an object among objects, and that the succession of his empirical perceptions depended on that of impressions of other objects on his body, and was therefore an objective succession. Such a succession takes place among objects *directly* (if not also indirectly) and independently of the subject's arbitrary choice, and so can be recognized quite easily without there being any causal connexion between the objects successively acting on his body.

Kant says that time cannot be perceived and hence that no succession of representations can be empirically perceived as objective, in other words, be distinguished as changes of phenomena from those of merely subjective representations. The objectivity of a change can be known only through the law of causality, i.e., through a rule in accordance with which states or conditions follow one another. And the result of his assertion would be that absolutely no succession in time is perceived by us as objective except that of cause and effect, and that every other succession of phenomena perceived by us is determined thus and not otherwise merely by our arbitrary choice. Against all this I must state that phenomena can quite easily *follow on one another* without *following from one another*. Nor is the law of causality prejudiced thereby; for it is still certain that every change is the effect of another change, since this truth is firmly established a priori; only that every change follows not merely on the single one that is its cause, but on all which exist simultaneously with that cause, and with which it stands in no casual relation. It is not perceived by me precisely in the sequence of causal succession, but in one quite different which, however, is nonetheless objective on that account and is very different from a subjective sequence that depends on my arbitrary choice, such for instance as the sequence of my phantasms. Events following on one another in time and standing in no causal connexion are precisely what is called *chance or contingency* (*Zufall*). This word is derived from *Zusammentreffen* (meeting together) or *Zusammenfallen* (falling together) of what is not connected, just as το συμβεβηκός is derived from συμβαίνειν. (Cf. Aristotle, *Posterier Analytics*, I, 4.) I go out of my house by the street door when a tile falls from the roof and strikes me; now there is no causal connexion between the falling of the tile and my going out, yet the succession, namely that my going out preceded the falling of the tile, is determined objectively in my apprehension, not subjectively by my arbitrary choice, which would normally prefer to have the succession reversed. In just the same way, the succession of sounds in a piece of music is determined objectively, not subjectively by me the listener; but who will say that the musical notes follow one another according to the law of cause and effect? In fact even the succession of day and night is undoubtedly known to us objectively, but they are certainly not regarded as cause and effect of each other; and before Copernicus everyone was mistaken as to their common cause without the correct knowledge of their succession being affected thereby. Incidentally, Hume's hypothesis is also refuted in this way, for the succession of day and night, the oldest and least liable to exception, has never misled anyone through custom or habit into regarding them as cause and effect of each other.

Elsewhere in his work Kant says that a representation shows objective reality (which, I suppose, means that it is distinguished from mere phantasms) only through our recognizing its necessary connexion—one that is tied to a rule (the casual law)—with other representations, and its place in a definite order of the time-relation of our representations. But of how few representations do we know the place assigned to them by the causal law in the series of causes and effects! Yet we are always able to distinguish objective representations from subjective, real objects from phantasms. In sleep where the brain is isolated from the peripheral nervous system and so from external impressions, we cannot make that distinction. Therefore while dreaming, we take phantasms for real objects, and only when we wake up, that is to say, when the sensible nerves and the outer world again enter consciousness, do we recognize the error, although even in the dream while it lasts the law of causality asserts its right, only that an impossible material is often assigned to it as a substitute. We might almost imagine that, in the above passage, Kant was under the influence of Leibniz, much as he was otherwise opposed to him in the whole of his philosophy, namely when it is observed that exactly similar statements are found in Leibniz's *New Essays Concerning Human Understanding* (Book IV, Chap. 2) [cf. Langley trans., Open Court ed., pp. 421-22 (editor's note)], e.g., "The truth of sensuous things consists only in the connexion of phenomena which must have its reason or ground, and this it is which distinguishes them from dreams. . . . The true criterion in respect of objects of the senses is the connexion of phenomena which guarantees the positive truths with regard to sensuous things outside us." [Tr.] [30]

With this entire proof of the a priori nature and necessity of the law of causality from the fact that only through its agency did we recognize the objective succession of changes, and that this law was to that extent the condition of experience, Kant obviously fell into a most curious error. This was so palpable that we can explain it only as a consequence of his becoming engrossed in the

Kantian mistake

a priori part of our knowledge, a circumstance which made him lose sight of that which everyone else could not fail to see. In § 21 I have given the only correct proof of the a priori nature of the law of causality which is at all times confirmed by the unshakable certainty with which everyone expects that experience will in all cases turn out in accordance with this law. In other words, the a priori nature is confirmed by the apodictic certainty which we attribute to this law and which differs from every other that is based on induction, e.g., from the certainty of empirically known natural laws, by the fact that we cannot even conceive anywhere in the world of experience an exception to this law. For example, we can *imagine* the law of gravitation ceasing to act at some time, but we could never conceive this as happening without a cause.

In their proofs Kant and Hume fell into opposite errors. Thus Hume declared all consequence to be mere sequence; Kant, on the other hand, affirmed that there is no other sequence but consequence. Pure understanding, of course, can comprehend only *consequence,* but it is no more capable of comprehending mere *sequence* than it is of comprehending the difference between right and left, which, like sequence, can be grasped only through pure sensibility. The sequence of events in time can certainly be known empirically (Kant denies this elsewhere in his work), just as the juxtaposition of things in space can be so known. But the *way in which* one thing generally *follows on* another in time can no more be explained than can the way in which one thing *follows from* another; the former knowledge is given and conditioned by pure sensibility, the latter by pure understanding. But by declaring that the objective sequence of phenomena can be known only through the guiding line of causality, Kant falls into the same error with which he reproaches Leibniz "for intellectualizing the forms of sensibility" (See *Critique of Pure Reason,* 1st ed., p. 275; 5th ed., p. 331.) The following is my view of succession. We draw our knowledge of the mere *possibility* of succession from the form of time that belongs to pure sensibility. The succession of real objects, the precise form of which is time, is known to us empirically and therefore as *actual.* But the *necessity* of a succession of two states, in other words, of a change, is known to us merely through the understanding by means of causality; and the fact that we are able to conceive the necessity of a succession at all, is already proof that the law of causality is not something empirically known, but given to us a priori. The principle of sufficient reason in general is the expression of the fundamental form at the very core of our cognitive faculty, namely the basic form of a necessary connexion between all our objects, i.e., our representations. This principle is the common form of all representations and the sole origin of the concept of *necessity*—a concept that has absolutely no other true substance or proof than that of the appearance of the consequent when its ground is established. In the class of representations here considered, where that principle appears as the law of causality, it determines the sequence in time. This is because time is the form of these representations, and so the necessary connexion appears here as the rule of succession. In the other forms of the principle of sufficient reason the necessary

130

connexion, everywhere demanded by it, will appear to us in forms quite different from that of time, and consequently not as succession. But it will always retain the character of a necessary connexion whereby the identity of the principle of sufficient reason in all its forms is revealed to us, or rather the unity of the root of all the laws, of which that principle is the expression.

If Kant's assertion were correct, which I challenge, our only way of knowing the *reality* of succession would be from its *necessity*; but this would presuppose an understanding embracing all the series of causes and effects simultaneously, and thus an omniscient understanding. Kant has burdened the understanding with an impossibility merely in order to have less need of sensibility.

How can we reconcile Kant's assertion that the objectivity of succession is known only from the necessity of the effect's following from its cause with his other assertion (*Critique of Pure Reason*, 1st ed., p. 203; 5th ed., p. 249), that succession is the empirical criterion as to which of two states is cause and which effect? Who does not see here the most obvious circle?

If objectivity of succession were known merely from causality, it would be conceivable only as such, and would be nothing but this. For if it were yet something different, it would also have other distinctive characteristics by which it could be recognized; but this is precisely what Kant denies. Consequently, if Kant were right, one could not say: "This state is the effect of that and hence follows it." On the contrary, following and being effect would be one and the same thing, and that proposition would be tautological. Therefore if the difference between sequence and consequence were abolished, Hume would again carry his point, for he declared all consequences to be mere sequence, and thus also denied that difference.

Kant's proof would therefore have to be reduced to saying that empirically we know only *reality* of succession. But as we know also *necessity* of succession in certain series of events, and know even prior to all experience, that every possible event must have a definite place in one or another of these series, the reality and the a priori nature of the law of causality follow from this. The only correct proof of the a priori nature of the causal law is the one given in § 21.

Parallel with Kant's theory that objective succession is possible and knowable only through the causal connexion, is the other that coexistence is possible and knowable only through reciprocity or reciprocal effect. They are given in the *Critique of Pure Reason* under the title of "Third Analogy of Experience." Here Kant goes to the length of saying "that the coexistence of phenomena which did not act reciprocally on one another, but were separated by, say, an empty space, would not be an object of possible perception" (this would be a proof a priori that there is no empty space between the fixed stars); and "that the light *playing between* our eye and heavenly bodies" (an expression surreptitiously introducing the notion that the light of the stars not only acts on our eyes, but that our eyes also act on it), "brings about a community between us and them, and thus proves the coexistence of the latter." Even empirically this last statement is false; for the sight of a fixed star by no means proves that it exists now simultaneously with the spectator, but at most that it existed a few, and in some cases thousands of, years ago. For the rest, this Kantian theory stands and falls with the first, only it can be much more easily seen through. Moreover, the invalidity of the whole concept of reciprocity has been discussed in § 20.

The argument here used against this Kantian proof may be compared with two previous attacks on it, namely Feder's in his book *Über Raum und Kausalität*, p. 29, and G. E. Schulze's in his *Kritik der theoretischen Philosophie*, Vol. II, p. 422 *et seq.*

It was not without much hesitation that I ventured (in 1813) to raise objections to a theory which had been generally accepted as proved, has been repeated even in the most recent works (e.,g., Fries, *Kritik der Vernunft*, Vol. II, p. 85), and is one of the principal theories of a man whose profound wisdom I admire and respect, and to whom I owe so much, that his spirit can say to me in the words of Homer: "I too removed the film that covered your eyes." (*Iliad*, V, 127. Tr.)[31]

§ 24. On the Improper Use of the Law of Causality

The result of our discussion so far is that we are guilty of such an abuse whenever we apply the law of causality to anything but *changes* in the material world that is given to us empirically. For example, it is an improper use of the causal law if we apply it to the forces of nature by virtue whereof such changes are at all possible; or if we apply it to matter *in* which they take place; or to the universe to which we must attribute in that case an absolutely objective existence that is not conditioned by our intellect. The causal law can also be misused in many other ways. I refer here to what has been said on this matter in the *World as Will and Representation*, Vol. II, Chap. 4. Such improper use always results from the fact that the concept *cause*, like very many others in metaphysics and morality, is taken in far *too wide* a sense, and also from our forgetting that the law of causality is indeed a presupposition which we bring with us into the world, and which renders possible the intuitive perception of things external to us. But for this very reason we are not justified in setting forth, as the absolute eternal order of the world and of all that exists, such a principle, outside and independently of the mechanism of our cognitive faculty from which it has sprung.

§ 25. The Time of a Change

As the principle of sufficient reason of becoming is applicable only to *changes*, we must not omit to mention that the philosophers of antiquity had already asked about the time in which a change takes place. Thus they asserted that a change cannot occur while the previous state still exists, nor can it occur after the new state has already come to pass. But if we give to the change its own time between the two states, then, during that time, a body could not possibly be either in the first state or in the second; thus for example, a dying man would be neither dead nor alive; a body would be neither at rest nor in motion, which would be absurd. The niceties and hair-splitting subtleties on this point are all found in Sextus Empiricus, *Adversus Mathematicos, Lib.* IX, 267-71, *et hypot.* III, c. 14; there is also something about them in Gellius, L. VI, c. 13. Plato had disposed of this difficult point rather offhandedly by asserting (in the *Parmenides,* p. 138 *Bip.*) that a change happens suddenly and occupies *no time at all.* He said that it is in the ἐξαίφης (*in repentino*),[32] which he calls "a strange existence that is not in any time," [Tr.][33] and thus a strange timeless existence (which nevertheless takes place in time).

Accordingly, it was left to Aristotle's penetrating mind to clear up this difficult matter, and this he did thoroughly and exhaustively in the sixth book of the *Physics,* Chap. 1-8. His proof that no change occurs suddenly (in Plato's ἐξαίφης),[32] but each takes place only gradually and thus occupies a certain time, is furnished entirely on the basis of the pure a priori intuition of time and space, but it also turns out to be very subtle. At all events, the essentials of this very long demonstration can be reduced to the following statements. Two things are adjacent or contiguous to each other is equivalent to saying that they have in common their opposite extreme ends; consequently

135

only two extended things, not two indivisible (for otherwise they would be one) can be adjacent to each other, and thus only lines and not mere points. This is now transferred from space to time. Just as there is always a line between two points, so is there still always a time between two nows. This is the time in which a change occurs, namely when one state is in the first now and the other in the second. Like any other, this time is infinitely divisible; and therefore that which changes in it passes through an infinite number of degrees, through which the second state gradually emerges from that *first*. The matter could be made more intelligible from the following explanation. Between two successive states whose difference is perceptible to our senses there are always several whose difference is not so perceptible because the newly appearing state must have reached a certain degree or size to be sensuously perceptible. It is therefore preceded by weaker degrees or smaller extensions, and by running through these it gradually emerges. Taken collectively, these are included under the name of change, and the time occupied by them is the time of change. If we apply this to a body that is being propelled, the first effect is a certain vibration of its inner parts, and, after the impulse has been transmitted through these, this effect breaks out into external motion. From the infinite divisibility of time Aristotle quite rightly infers that everything filling time and consequently every change, i.e., every transition from one state to another, must also be infinitely divisible, and hence that everything coming into existence, is in fact assembled from an infinite number of parts, and consequently comes about always gradually and

Aristotle agreement w/ concerning Kant time in Causality

never suddenly. From the above principles, and from the gradual arising of every movement which follows therefrom, he draws the important conclusion in the last chapter of that book that nothing indivisible and consequently no mere *point* can move. This agrees very well with Kant's explanation of matter as "that which is movable in space."

This law of the continuity and gradualness of all changes, first laid down and established by Aristotle, is found explained three times by Kant in his *Dissertatio de mundi sensibilis et intelligibilis forma,* § 14, then in the *Critique of Pure Reason,* 1st ed., p. 207, and 5th ed., p. 253, and finally in the *Metaphysical First Principles of Natural Science* at the end of the "General Note on Mechanics." In all three his statement of the case is brief, but yet not so thorough as Aristotle's; substantially, however, the two statements agree entirely. There is therefore little doubt that Kant obtained these ideas directly or indirectly from Aristotle, although he does not mention him anywhere. Aristotle's proposition—"It cannot possibly be assumed that moments are contiguous to one another, as one point is to others" [Tr.][34]—is here found expressed as follows: "between two moments there is always a time," to which it may be objected that "even between two centuries there is no time because in time, as in space, there must be a pure limit." Therefore, instead of mentioning Aristotle in the first and earliest of the above statements, Kant tries to identify the theory advanced by him with the *lex continuitatis* of Leibniz. If the two were really the same, Leibniz would have had the whole thing from Aristotle. Now Leibniz first stated this *loi de la continuité* (according to his own account on page 189 of the *Opera philosophica,* ed. Erdmann) in a letter to Bayle (*ibid.,* p. 104), where he nevertheless calls it *principe de l'ordre général.* Under this name he gives a very general, vague, and mainly geometrical line of argument; and this has no direct reference to the time of change which he does not mention at all.

1. Cf. *Critique of Pure Reason,* Elementary Theory, Sec. II, Conclusions from the Arguments b and c. P. 33 of the first edition, p. 49 of the fifth.

Translator's addition: In Prof. Max Müller's English translation the pagination of the original German text of the first edition is given in the English text in square brackets.

2. Κατ' ἐξοχήν.

3. Κατ' ἐντελέχειαν.

4. Κατὰ δύναμιν.

5. *Harmonia praestabilita,* "pre-established harmony" — a fundamental conception of the philosophy of Leibniz. According to its dynamism matter and spirit, body and soul, the physical and the moral, each a "windowless" perfect monad in itself, are once and for all not only corresponding realities, but are also synchronized by God in their changes like two clocks, thus rendering nugatory the assumption of any mutual or other influences. [Tr.]

6. Κατ' ἐξοχήν.

7. *Causa est principium, a quo existentia sive actualitas entis alterius dependet.*

8. "A logical inconsistency between a noun and its modifying adjective" [such as "a round square," "wooden iron," "cold fire," "hot snow." Tr.]

9. Goethe's *Der Zauberlehrling.* [Tr.]

10. An enthymeme is a syllogism one of whose premisses or the conclusion is not explicitly stated.

A prosyllogism is a syllogism that proves or furnishes a reason for one of the premisses of another syllogism. [Tr.]

11. Old students' song. [Tr.]

12. "According to plan"; i.e., where Kant deals expressly with this proof. [Tr.]

13. "Reason or cause." [Tr.]

14. Here used in the absolute sense of *liberum arbitrium indifferentiae;* liberty of indifference, or the power to determine the will at pleasure in any given direction; perfect freedom in the *choice* of our manner of acting. [Tr.]

15. "Whatever conception we may form of the freedom of the will for metaphysical purposes, its phenomena, namely

human actions, are nevertheless determined according to universal laws of nature, just as are all other events in nature." *Ideas of a Universal History*. The beginning.

"All man's actions in the phenomenon are determined from his empirical character and other concomitant causes, according to the order of nature; and if we could investigate to the very bottom all the phenomena of his will, there would not be a single human action which we could not predict with certainty and recognize as necessary from its preceding conditions. Hence there is no freedom with regard to this empirical character, and yet it is only in accordance therewith that we can consider man when we merely observe and, as is done in anthropology, try to investigate physiologically from his actions the causes that move him." *Critique of Pure Reason*, p. 548 of the first edition, and p. 577 of the fifth.

"It can therefore be taken for granted that, if it were possible for us to have so deep an insight into a man's way of thinking, as manifested by his inner as well as his outer actions, that every motive, even the slightest, were known to us, likewise all the external causes acting on this, it would be possible for us to calculate a man's future conduct with the same certainty with which we calculate an eclipse of the moon or sun." *Critique of Practical Reason*, p. 230 of Rosenkranz's edition, and p. 177 of the fourth.

16. "Hush, hush!" [Tr.]

17. Δός μοι ποῦ στῶ.

18. In the chapter "Physiology and Pathology." [Tr.]

19. *Vernunft* is derived from *vernehmen* which means to become aware of, to learn (by hearing), to understand, to hear (and thus understand). [Tr.]

*The *Frankfurter Konversationsblatt* of 22 July 1853 gives an account of this man: "On 10 July the blind sculptor Joseph Kleinhanns died at Nauders (Tyrol). Losing his sight through cow-pox when he was five, the boy played about and carved for pastime. Prugg gave him instruction and figures to copy, and in his twelfth year the boy finished a Christ in life size. In the workshop of the sculptor Nissel at Fügen he profited very much in a short time and, by virtue of his abilities and talents, became the well-known sculptor. His works are very numerous and of different kinds. His images of Christ alone number four hundred, and in these his masterly skill is apparent, if we take into account his blindness. He also sculptured other objects worthy of recognition, and only two months ago made a bust of the Emperor Francis Joseph which was sent to Vienna."

[Footnotes so marked (with an asterisk) represent additions made by Schopenhauer in his interleaved copy of the second edition between its appearance in 1847 and his death in 1860. Tr.]

20. "Internal changes of the eye." [Tr.]

21. Feuerbach's *Caspar Hauser—Beispiel eines Verbrechens am Seelenleben eines Menschen*, Anspach, 1832, p. 79 *et seq.*

22. Haslam's *Observations on Madness and Melancholy*, 2d ed., p. 192.

23. "*Il faut faire une grande distinction entre les sens et l'intelligence. L'ablation d'un tubercle détermine la perte de la SENSATION, du SENS de la vue; la rétine devient insensible, l'iris devient immobile. L'ablation d'un lobe cérébral laisse la SENSATION, le SENS, la SENSIBILITÉ de la rétine, la MOBILITÉ de l'iris; elle ne détruit que la PERCEPTION seule. Dans un cas, c'est un fait SENSORIAL; et dans l'autre, un fait CÉRÉBRAL; dans un cas, c'est la perte du SENS; dans l'autre, c'est la perte de la PERCEPTION. La distinction des perceptions et des sensations est encore un grand résultat; et il est démontré aux yeux. Il y a deux moyens de faire perdre la vision par l'encephale: (1) par les tubercles, c'est la perte du sens, de la sensation; (2) par les lobes, c'est la perte de la perception, de l'intelligence. La sensibilité n'est donc pas l'intelligence, penser n'est donc pas sentir; et voilà toute une philosophie renversée. L'idée n'est donc pas la sensation; et voilà encore une autre preuve du vice radical de cette philosophie.*" ... "*Il y a une de mes expériences qui sépare*

nettement la SENSIBILITE de la PERCEPTION. Quand on enlève le CERVEAU PROPREMENT DIT (LOBES ou HÉMISPHÈRES CÉRÉBRAUX) à un animal, l'animal perd la vue. Mais, par rapport à l'oeil, rien n'est changé: les objets continuent à se peindre sur la rétine; l'IRIS reste contractile, le NERF OPTIQUE sensible, parfaitement sensible. Et cependant l'animal ne voit plus; il n'y a plus VISION, quoique tout ce qui est SENSATION subsiste; il n'y a plus VISION, parce qu'il n'y a plus PERCEPTION. Le PERCEVOIR, et non le SENTIR, est donc le premier élément de l'INTELLIGENCE. La PERCEPTION est partie de l'INTELLIGENCE, car elle se perd avec l'INTELLIGENCE, et par l'ablation du même organe, les LOBES ou HÉMISPHÈRES CÉRÉBRAUX; et la SENSIBILITÉ n'en est point partie, puisqu'elle subsiste après la perte de l'INTELLIGENCE et l'ablation des LOBES ou HÉMISPHÈRES."

24. Νοῦς ὁρῇ καὶ νοῦς ἀκούει· τ'ἄλλα κωφὰ καὶ τυφλά. *(Mens videt, mens audit; caetera surda et coeca.)*

25. Ὡς τοῦ περὶ τὰ ὄμματα καὶ ὦτα πάθους, ἂν μὴ παρῇ τὸ φρονοῦν, αἴσθησιν οὐ ποιοῦντος. *(Quia affectio oculorum et aurium nullum affert sensum, intelligentia absente.)*

26. Στράτωνος τοῦ φυσικοῦ λόγος ἐστίν ἀποδεικνύων ὡς οὐδ'αἰσθάνεσθαι τὸ παράπαν ἄνευ τοῦ νοεῖν ὑπάρχει.*(Stratonis physici exstat ratiocinatio, qua "sine intelligentia sentiri omnino nihil posse" demonstrat.)*

27. Ὅθεν ἀνάγκη, πᾶσιν, οἷς τὸ αἰσθάνεσθαι, μὰι τὸ νοεῖν ὑπάρχειν, εἰ τῷ νοεῖν αἰσθάνεσθαι πεφύκαμεν *(quare necesse est, omnia quae sentiunt, etiam intelligere, siquidem intelligendo demum sentiamus).*

28. Εὔμαιε, τὸ σοφόν ἐστιν οὐ καθ'ἕν μόνον, Ἀλλ' ὅσα περ ζῇ, πάντα καὶ γνώμαν ἔχει. *(Eumaee, sapientia non uni tantum competit, sed quaecunque vivunt etiam intellectum habent).*

29. The German is *Wissenschaftsleere* (emptiness of science), a word used by Schopenhauer as a pun on *Wissenschaftslehre (Doctrine of Science),* the title of a work by Fichte. [Tr.]

30. *La vérité des choses sensibles ne consiste que dans la liaison des phénomènes, qui doit avoir sa raison, et c'est ce qui les distingue des songes, ... Le vrai Critérion, en matière des objets des sens, est la liaison des phénomènes qui garantit les vérités de fait, à l'égard des choses sensibles hors de nous.*

31. Ἀχλὺν δ'αὖ τοι ἀπ' ὀφθαλμῶν ἕλον, ἢ πρὶν ἐπῆεν.

32. "Suddenly." [Tr.]

33. Ἄτοπος φύσις, ἐν χρόνῳ οὐδὲν οὖσα.

34. Οὐκ ἔστιν ἀλλήλων ἐχόμενα τὰ νῦν.

Human reason
affords concepts
which in turn
are abstract representations

CHAPTER V

ON THE SECOND CLASS OF OBJECTS FOR THE SUBJECT AND THE FORM OF THE PRINCIPLE OF SUFFICIENT REASON RULING THEREIN

§ 26. Explanation of This Class of Objects

The only essential difference between human being and animal, which from time immemorial has been attributed to the *faculty of reason* (*Vernunft*), a very special cognitive faculty belonging exclusively to man, is based on the fact that he has a class of representations not shared by any animal. They are *concepts* and thus *abstract* representations, as opposed to the representations of intuitive perception, from which they are nevertheless drawn off. The direct consequence of this is that the animal neither speaks nor laughs; but the indirect consequences are all the many important things distinguishing human life from that of the animal. For by the addition of the abstract representation, motivation has also assumed a different character. Although man's actions ensue with a necessity as strict as that with which the actions of animals follow, through motivation of this kind, insofar as it here consists of *thoughts and ideas* that render possible an *elective decision* (i.e., the conscious conflict of motives), action with a purpose, with deliberation according to plans and maxims and in agreement with others and so on, has nevertheless taken the place of the mere impulse through objects that lie before us in intuitive perception. But this gives rise to all that makes man's life so rich, artificial, and terrible that in the West where his skin has turned white and whither he has not been able to bring the old, true, profound, and original religions of his first fatherland, he no longer recognizes his brother. On the contrary, he imagines that the animals are something fundamentally different and, to strengthen this erroneous idea, calls them beasts or brutes, gives degrading names to all the vital functions they have in common with him, and says they have no rights, in that he forces himself not to see that identity between his own true nature and theirs which obtrudes itself on him.

However, as I have said, the whole difference consists in the fact that, besides the representations of intuitive perception, considered in the last chapter and shared also by the animals, man harbours in his brain, which is mainly for this purpose so much more voluminous, abstract representations drawn from those of intuitive perception. Such abstract representations have been called *concepts* (*Begriffe*), since each conceives or grasps (*begreift*) in (or rather under) itself innumerable individual things, and hence is a *complex or comprehensive totality* (*Inbegriff*) thereof. They can also be defined as *representations from representations.* For in their formation the faculty of abstraction analyses the complete and therefore intuitive representations, dealt with in the previous chapter, into their component parts in order to be able to think of these

146

separately, each by itself, as the different qualities of, or relations between, things. But in this process the representations necessarily forfeit their perceptibility, just as water ceases to be a visible liquid when it is decomposed into its elements. For every quality thus isolated (abstracted) may indeed be *conceived* alone by itself, yet not on that account be also *perceived* alone by itself. The formation of a concept is brought about generally by dropping much that is given in intuitive perception in order then to be able to think of what is left by itself. The concept is therefore a case of thinking less than what is intuitively perceived. If, when considering various objects of intuitive perception, we have dropped something different from each, and have yet retained what is the same in all, then this is the *genus* of that species. Accordingly, the concept of every *genus* is that of every species conceived or comprised under it, after the deduction of all that does not belong to *all* the species. Now every possible concept can be thought of as a *genus*; hence it is always something general, and as such cannot be intuitively perceived. Therefore a concept also has a *sphere* which is the complex or comprehensive totality (*Inbegriff*) of all that may be thought through it. The higher we ascend in abstraction, the more we drop, and so the less there remains for us to think. The highest, i.e., the most general, concepts are the emptiest and poorest, and ultimately are mere husks, such as, being, essence, thing, becoming, and the like. Incidentally, what can be achieved with philosophical systems which are merely spun out of concepts of this sort, and have for their material only such flimsy husks of thoughts? They are bound to be exceedingly empty, poor, and must therefore prove to be insufferably tedious.

Now since, as I have said, the representations, sublimated and thereby analysed into abstract concepts, have forfeited all perceptibility, they would slip entirely from consciousness and be absolutely of no avail for the thought operations it intended therewith, if they were not fixed and retained in our senses by arbitrary signs. Such signs are words, and therefore insofar as words constitute the contents of dictionaries and hence of language, they always express *universal* representations, concepts, never the things of intuitive perception. On the other hand, a lexicon, enumerating individual things, does not contain words, but only proper names. It is either a geographical or historical lexicon; in other words, it enumerates what is separated either by time or space, since as *my* readers know, time and space are the *principium individuationis.* Merely because animals are limited to representations of intuitive perception and are incapable of any abstraction and consequently of forming any concept, they have no language, even when they are able to pronounce words; on the other hand, they understand proper names. It is clear from my theory of the ludicrous, given in the first book of the *World as Will and Representation,* § 13 and in volume two, chaper eight, that the same shortcoming excludes animals from laughter.

If we analyse the long and continuous speech of a wholly uneducated man, we find in it an abundance of logical forms, constructions, turns of phrase, distinctions, and subtleties of every kind, correctly expressed by means of grammatical forms and their inflexions and constructions, even with the frequent application of the *sermo obliquus,* of the different moods of the verb, and so on, everything according to rules. All this astonishes us, and here we are bound to see a very extensive and coherent branch of learning. But this knowledge has been acquired on the basis of our apprehending the world of intuitive perception, and to reduce the whole essence of such a world to abstract concepts is the fundamental business of the faculty of reason, a function that it can carry out only by means of language. Therefore in the mastering of a language the whole mechanism of the reasoning faculty, all that is essential in logic, is brought into consciousness. Obviously this cannot take place without great mental effort and close attention, for which the desire to learn endows children with the requisite strength. Such a desire is strong if it has before it what is genuinely useful and necessary, and appears weak only when we try to force on the child what is unsuitable and inappropriate. Hence in mastering a language together with all its subtleties and turns of phrase, even an ill-bred and uncultured child, by listening to his own speech and that of adults, achieves that development of his reasoning faculty, and acquires that genuinely concrete logic. This does not consist in logical rules, but directly in their correct application, just as one musically gifted learns the rules of harmony through merely playing the piano by ear without reading the notes and studying thorough-bass. The deaf and dumb, however, do not go through the above-mentioned logical training through the acquisition of speech, and so are almost as irrational as the animal, if they do not receive, by learning to read, that suitable and very artificial instruction which for them becomes the substitute for the natural training of the reasoning faculty.

§ 27. The Use of Concepts

As I have shown already, the fundamental essence of our reasoning or thinking faculty is that of abstraction, or the ability to form *concepts*. It is therefore the presence of these in consciousness which produces such astonishing results. That it is able to do this is due essentially to the following.

By the very fact that concepts contain less than the representations from which they have been abstracted, they are easier to deal with than these. Concepts are related to representations in much the same way as the formulae in higher arithmetic are to the mental operations whereof they are the result and which they represent, or as the logarithm is to its number. Of the many representations from which they are drawn, they contain only that part which is being used. If, instead of this, we tried to call to mind through the imagination those representations themselves, we should have to trail round a load of unessential material, as it were; and this would result in confusion. But through the application of concepts we think of only those parts and relations of all those representations which are required for each particular purpose. Accordingly, their use can be compared to getting rid of unnecessary baggage, or even to working with extracts instead of the plant species themselves, with quinine instead of the bark. What is properly called *thinking* in the narrower sense is the occupation of the intellect with *concepts*, the presence in our consciousness of that class of representations here considered. It is also expressed by the word *reflection* which, as a metaphor from optics, at the same time states the derived and secondary character of this kind of knowledge. Now this thinking, this reflection, imparts to man that *sober reflectiveness* which is wanting in the animal. For since it enables him to think of a thousand things through one concept. but always only what is essential in each, he can at will drop differences of every kind, and thus even those of space and time. In this way he acquires the power to survey in thought the past and future as well as what is absent, whereas the animal is in every respect tied to the present. Again this reflectiveness, the ability to *reflect or deliberate,* to come to his senses, is really the root of all man's theoretical and practical achievements by which he eclipses the animal. It is in the first place the basis of his concern for the future having regard for the past, then of the intentional, systematic, and methodical procedure in every scheme, of the cooperation of many people for a single purpose, and hence of law, order, the State, and so on. But concepts are particularly the proper material of the sciences whose aims may be utimately reduced to knowledge of the particular through the general. Such knowledge is possible only by means of the *dictum de omni et nullo,*[1] and this again only through the existence of concepts. Therefore Aristotle says: "For without the universal, knowledge is impossible." [Tr.][2] (*Metaphysics,* XII, c. 9.) Concepts are just those *universalia* whose mode of existence was the argument of the controversy in the Middle Ages between realists and nominalists.

[handwritten: Concept — Thought, notion, — ability of mind to distinguish one thing from another or universals abstracted from particulars]

§ 28. Representatives of Concepts. The Power of Judgement

As I have said, the concept is not to be confused with the phantasm in general, as this is an intuitive, complete, and thus individual representation; yet it is not brought about directly through an impression on the senses, and so does not belong to the complex of experience. But even when the phantasm is used *as the representative of a concept,* it should be distinguished therefrom. This occurs when we wish to have the intuitive representation itself from which the concept has sprung, and indeed to have it corresponding thereto, which is always impossible. There is, for example, no representation of dog in general, of colour, triangle, or number in general; there is no phantasm corresponding to these. We then conjure up the phantasm possibly of some dog which as representation must be determined throughout, in other words, have a certain size, a definite form, colour, and so on; yet the concept whereof the dog is a representative has no such determinations. Nevertheless, when using such a representative of a concept, we are always conscious that it is not adequate to the concept represented thereby, but is full of arbitrary

[handwritten: Judgement - deliberate function of consciousness involving identifying comparing discriminating and evaluating whereby values and knowledge are asserted]

determinations. Hume in his *Essays on Human Understanding*, Essay 12, Part 1 towards the end, and likewise Rousseau in the middle of the first part of *Sur l'origine de l'inégalité*, express agreement with what is said here. On the other hand, Kant teaches on this point something quite different in the chapter of the schematism of the pure concepts of the understanding. Only inner observation and clear reflection can decide the matter. Accordingly, everyone should find out whether in his concepts he is conscious of a "monogram of pure imagination a priori"; when, for example, he thinks of dog, whether he is conscious of something *entre chien et loup*,[3] or whether according to the explanations here given he either thinks of a concept through his faculty of reason, or through his imagination represents as a complete picture some representative of the concept.

All thinking in the wider sense, and hence all inner activity of the mind generally requires either words or pictures of the imagination; without the one or the other it has no support. But both are not required simultaneously, although they can work in together for mutual support. Thinking in the narrower sense, abstract thinking carried out with the aid of words, is either purely logical reasoning, where it then keeps entirely to its own sphere; or it borders on the representations of intuitive perception in order to come to an understanding with them for the purpose of connecting the empirically given and intuitively grasped with clearly thought out abstract concepts, so as to have complete possession thereof. Consequently, thinking seeks either the concept for the given case of intuitive perception, or the rule to which the case belongs; or else it seeks the case for the given concept or rule, the case that proves the rule. In this capacity thinking is an activity of the *power of judgement*, and indeed (according to Kant's subdivision) in the first case a reflecting, and in the second a subsuming, activity. Accordingly, the power of judgement is the mediator between knowledge of intuitive perception and abstract knowledge, or between the understanding and the faculty of reason. With most people the power of judgement is only rudimentary and often only of nominal existence;[4] their destiny is to be led by others, and one should not speak to them more than is necessary.

The real kernel of all knowledge is reflection or thinking that operates with the help of representations of intuitive perception, since it goes back to the primary source, the foundation, of all concepts. It is therefore the generator of all genuinely original ideas, of all primary and fundamental views and inventions, insofar as it was not chance that had the largest share therein. In this thinking the *understanding* is predominantly active, as is the *faculty of reason* in the other purely abstract thinking. Certain ideas belong to it which run for a long time through our heads, come and go, and are clothed now in one intuition now in another until they become clear, are fixed in concepts, and find words to express them. Indeed, there are some which never find words, and alas these are the best; *quae voce meliora sunt,*[5] as Apuleius says.

But Aristotle went too far in thinking that no reflection can take place without pictures of the imagination. Nevertheless his remarks on this point in the works *De*

154

*what about gravity ?
ball falling to earth*

anima (III, c. c. 3, 7, 8), such as "The soul never thinks without a picture of the imagination"; and "when we think of something, we must at the same time think in addition a picture of the imagination"; likewise *De memoria*, c. 1, "thinking is impossible without a picture of the imagination"; [Tr.]⁶ `made a great impression on the thinkers of the fifteenth and sixteenth centuries who thus frequently and emphatically repeated them. For instance, Pico della Mirandola says in *De imaginatione*, c. 5: "Whoever reflects and thinks must (according to Aristotle) necessarily look at pictures of the imagination"; Melanchthon (*De anima*, p. 130) says: "Whoever thinks must at the same time look at pictures of the imagination"; and Giordano Bruno says (*De compositione imaginum*, p. 10), "Aristotle says that whoever wants to know something must look at pictures of the imagination." [Tr.]⁷ Pomponatius (*De immortalitate*, p. 54 and p. 70) expresses himself in this sense. This much may be affirmed, that every true and original piece of knowledge and every geniune philosopheme must have as their innermost kernel and root some intuitive apprehension. Although momentary and single, this subsequently imparts spirit and life to the whole analysis, however detailed, just as one drop of the right reagent imparts to the whole solution the colour of the resultant precipitate. If the analysis has such a kernel, it is like the note of a bank able to pay in cash. On the other hand, every other analysis that has sprung from mere combinations of concepts is like the note of a bank which for security has again merely deposited other promissory notes. All purely rational talk is thus an elucidation of what follows from given concepts, and so does not really bring anything new to light. It could therefore be left to everyone to do for himself, instead of being put every day into large volumes.

§ 29. Principles of Sufficient Reason of Knowing

Yet even thinking and reflection in the narrower sense do not consist in the mere presence of abstract concepts in our consciousness, but rather in a combining or separating of two or more concepts under various restrictions and modifications, which are specified by logic in the theory of judgements. Thus such a concept relationship clearly conceived and expressed is called a *judgement*. Now with regard to these judgements, here the principle of sufficient reason once again holds good, yet in a form very different from the one discussed in the previous chapter, namely as the principle of sufficient reason of knowing, *principium rationis sufficientis cognoscendi*. As such it asserts that, if a judgement is to express a piece of *knowledge*, it must have a sufficient ground or reason (Grund); by virtue of this quality, it then receives the predicate *true*. *Truth* is therefore the reference of a judgement to something different therefrom. This something is called the ground or reason of the judgement and, as we shall see, itself admits of a considerable variety of classes. But as it is always something on which the judgement is supported or rests, the German word *Grund* (ground) is suitably chosen. In

Latin and all languages derived therefrom, the words *ground of knowledge* (*Erkenntnissgrund*) are identical with the word *reason* (*Vernunft*). Hence the two are called *ratio, la ragione, la razon, la raison, the reason.* From this it is evident that, in knowledge of the grounds of judgements, one recognized the principal function of reason (*Vernunft*) its business "par excellence." [Tr.] [8] These grounds whereon a judgement can be based may now be divided into four kinds, and then the truth gained through the judgement is different according to each of the four kinds. These are stated in the four follow.ng paragraphs.

4 bases of Judgement

§ 30. Logical Truth

A judgement can have as its reason or ground another judgement; its truth is then *logical* or *formal.* Whether it also has material truth remains undecided and depends on whether the judgement supporting it has material truth, or even whether the series of judgements, on which this judgement is based, leads back to one that has material truth. Such an establishment of one judgement by another results always from a comparison therewith. Now this comparison is made either directly in the mere conversion or contraposition of the judgement, or by the addition of a third judgement, where from the mutual relation of the last two judgements the truth of the judgement to be established becomes evident. This operation is the complete *syllogism.* It is brought about both by the subsumption and the opposition of concepts. The syllogism, as the establishment of one judgement through another by means of a third, is always concerned only with judgements which are merely combinations of concepts, and concepts are the exclusive object of the faculty of reason. Therefore arguing, concluding, or inferring has rightly been regarded as the proper and particular business of the faculty of reason (*Vernunft*). The whole science of syllogisms is nothing but the sum-total of rules for applying the principle of sufficient reason mutually to judgements; and so it is the canon of *logical truth.*

Those judgements whose truth is evident from the four well-known laws of thought can also be regarded as established by another judgement; for those four laws are themselves judgements from which the truth of the other judgements follows. For example, the judgement: "A Triangle is a space enclosed by three lines" has as its ultimate ground the principle of identity, in other words, the idea expressed by that principle. The judgement "No body is without extension" has as its ultimate ground the principle of contradiction. The judgement "Every judgement is either true or not true" has as its ultimate ground the principle of the excluded middle. Finally, the judgement "No one can admit anything to be true without knowing why" has as its ultimate ground the principle of sufficient reason of knowing. In the ordinary use of our faculty of reason we assume as true the judgements that follow from the four laws of thought, without first reducing them to those laws as their premisses, for indeed most people have never even heard of those abstract laws. This does not make those judgements any more independent of these laws as their premisses, just as when anyone says "this body will fall if its support is removed," such judgement is possible without his ever having been aware of the principle "all bodies tend towards the centre of the earth," and yet the former judgement is dependent on the latter as its premiss. I therefore cannot approve that hitherto in logic an *intrinsic truth* was attributed to all judgements based exclusively on the laws of thought, in other words, that they were declared to be *directly true*, and this *intrinsic logical truth* was distinguished from *extrinsic logical truth*, which would be reliance on another judgement as their ground. Every truth is the reference of a judgement to something *outside* it, and *intrinsic truth* is a contradiction.

§ 31. Empirical Truth

A representation of the first class, thus an intuitive perception brought about by means of the senses, and consequently experience, can be the ground of a judgement which then has *material* truth; and indeed insofar as the judgement is founded *directly* on experience, this is *empirical truth.*

A judgement has *material truth* implies generally that its concepts are mutually connected, separated, or limited, as is required by the intuitive representations through

159

which it is established. To know this is the immediate business of the *power of judgement* which, as I have said, is the mediator between the intuitive and abstract or discursive faculties of knowledge, and thus between understanding and faculty of reason.

§ 32. Transcendental Truth

The *forms* of intuitive empirical knowledge, to be found in the understanding and pure sensibility, can, as conditions of the possibility of all experience, be the ground of a judgement, which is then synthetical a priori. But as such a judgement has material truth, this is transcendental, since the judgement rests not merely on experience but on the conditions of the entire possiblity of experience which lie within us. For the judgement is determined precisely by that which determines experience itself, that is, either by the forms of space and time intuitively perceived by us a priori, or by the law of causality known to us a priori. Examples of such judgements are propositions such as: two straight lines do not enclose a space.—Nothing happens without a cause.— 3 x 7 = 21.—Matter can neither come into existence nor pass away. The whole of pure mathematics, as well as my table of the *Praedicabilia a priori* in the second volume of the *World as Will and Representation*, and also most of the propositions in Kant's *Metaphysical Rudiments of Natural*

160

Science, can be quoted as evidence of this kind of truth.

§ 33. Metalogical Truth

Finally, the formal conditions of all thought which lie within our faculty of reason can also be the ground of a judgement, and then its truth is such that I think this is best defined when I call it *metalogical truth*. But this expression has nothing to do with the *Metalogicus*, written in the twelfth century by Johannes Saresberiensis; for in his *prologus* he explains: "Because I support and defend logic, my book is called *Metalogicus*," [Tr.][9] and makes no further use of the word. There are, however, only four such judgements of metalogical truth which were found long ago by induction and called the laws of all thought, although complete agreement about their expression and number has never yet been reached, but there is, of course, complete unanimity about what they are supposed to indicate. They are: (1) A subject is equal to the sum of its predicates, or $a = a$. (2) No predicate can be simultaneously attributed and denied to a subject, or $a = - a = 0$. (3) Of every two contradictorily opposite predicates one must belong to every subject. (4) Truth is the reference of a judgement to something outside it as its sufficient ground or reason.

Through a reflection, which I might call a self-examination of the faculty of reason, we know that these judgements are the expression of the conditions of all

Reason compels us not to think of metalogical truths in their opposite truths

thought and therefore have these as their ground. Thus by making vain attempts to think in opposition to these laws, the faculty of reason recognizes them as the conditions of the possibility of all thought. We then find that it is just as impossible to think in opposition to them as it is to move our limbs in a direction contrary to their joints. If the subject could know itself, we should know those laws *immediately*, and not first through experiments on objects, i.e. representations. In this respect it is just the same with the grounds of judgements of transcendental truth; they too do not come directly into our consciousness, but first *in concreto* by means of objects, i.e., representations. For example, if we attempt to think of a change without a preceding cause, or even of an arising or passing away of matter, we become aware of the impossibility of the business, indeed of an objective impossiblity, although it has its roots in our intellect; otherwise we could not bring it to consciousness in a subjective way. Generally a great similarity and connexion between transcendental and metalogical truths is noticeable, which shows that both have a common root. Here we see the principle of sufficient reason mainly as metalogical truth, after it had appeared in the previous chapter as transcendental truth. In the next chapter it will again appear as transcendental truth in another form. Precisely on this account I am attempting in this essay to establish the principle of sufficient reason as a judgement having a fourfold ground or reason. By this I do not mean four different grounds or reasons leading by chance to the same judgement, but one ground or reason presenting itself in a fourfold aspect, which I call figura-

transcendental and metalogical truths have a common root in the principle of sufficient reason

tively a fourfold root. The other three metalogical truths are so similar that, when considering them, we attempt almost of necessity to seek for them a common expression, as I have done in the ninth chapter of the second volume of my chief work. On the other hand, they are very different from the principle of sufficient reason. If we wished to seek among the transcendental truths an analogue for those other three metalogical truths, the one to be chosen would be: Substance, I mean matter, is permanent.

§ 34. The Faculty of Reason (*Vernunft*)

The class of representations considered in this chapter belongs to man alone, and all that distinguishes his life so forcibly from that of animals, and gives him so great an advantage over them, rests, as we have shown, on his capacity for such representations. This, then, obviously and unquestionably constitutes that *faculty of reason* which from time immemorial has been extolled as man's prerogative. Likewise all that has been regarded at all times and by all nations as the express manifestation or work of reason, λόγος, λογικός, λογιστικόν, *ratio, la ragione, la razon, la raison, Vernunft, reason*, is evidently reduced to what is possible only to abstract, discursive, reflective, and mediate knowledge that is tied to words, but not to what is possible to merely intuitive, immediate, and sensuous knowledge, which animals also share. Cicero quite rightly associates *ratio et oratio (De Officiis, I, 16)*, and describes them as "reason and speech which by teaching, learning, communicating, negotiating, and judging make for friendship among men," and so on. Likewise (*De natura deorum*, II, 7), "I call this reason, or, if you want more words, mind, deliberation, thinking, circumspection." Also (*De legibus*, I, 10): "Reason which constitutes our only advantage over the animals, and by which we have the power to foresee, to prove, to refute, to demonstrate, to discover something, to arrive at a decision." [Tr.]^{10} All philosophers down to Kant have everywhere and at all times spoken of reason (*Vernunft*) in this sense. Moreover, even Kant himself defines it as the faculty of principles and inference, although it is undeniable that he was responsible for the subsequent misinterpretations. I have already spoken at length of the agreement of all philosophers on this point, and about the true nature of the faculty of reason, as opposed to the false notion professors of philosophy have of it in the nineteenth century (see *World as Will and Representation*, Vol. I, § 8, also the Appendix; and again Vol. II, Chap. 6; finally *The Two Fundamental Problems of Ethics*, "Basis of Morality," § 6). Therefore I need not repeat here all that has been said in those works, but confine myself to the following remarks.

The professors of philosophy have deemed it advisable to abolish the name previously given to that faculty of thinking and consideration by means of reflection and concepts. This faculty distinguishes man from the animals, requires language and enables us to use this, is the basis of man's deliberation and of all his achievements, and therefore has always been looked at in this way and taken in this sense by all nations and even by all philosophers. Now in defiance of all usage of language and of sound judgement, the professors have decided to call the thinking faculty *understanding* instead of *reason* (*Vernunft*), and likewise everything springing therefrom *intelligent* instead of *rational*; but then this was bound always to lead to a strange and awkward result, like a false note in music. For the words *understanding, intellectus, acumen, perspicacia, sagacitas,* and so on were used always and everywhere to denote the immediate and more intuitive faculty discussed in the previous chapter; and the results, springing therefrom and specifically different from the rational results we are now considering, were called intelligent, sagacious, clever, and so on. Accordingly, intelligent and rational were always entirely different, as expressions of two wholly and widely different mental faculties. But the professors of philosophy were not at liberty to take this into account, for their policy called for this sacrifice, and in such cases they said: "Move on, truth; we have higher, well-conceived plans in view! Truth, stand aside *in majorem Dei gloriam,*[11] as you have long been in the habit of doing! Do you pay fees and salaries? Move on, truth, move on; go to merit and squat down in the corner!" Thus they needed the place and name of *reason* (*Vernunft*) for an invented and fabricated, or more correctly and honestly, a wholly fictitious, faculty that would help them out of the straits to which Kant had reduced them. It is said to be one of immediate metaphysical knowledge, that is to say, one that transcends all possibility of experience, and grasps the world of things-in-themselves and their relations. Accord-

165

ingly, it is a faculty which is primarily a "consciousness of God," in other words, has direct knowledge of the Lord, constructs a priori the way in which he created the world, or, should this be too trivial, the way in which he sent it forth from himself, and to a certain extent brought it forth through a more or less necessary vital process. Or again, what is most convenient, although extremely comical, this faculty can construct the way in which God "dismissed" the world according to the custom and tradition of the nobility at the end of an audience, for then it can get on to its legs by itself and go off whither it pleases. For this last step, of course, only the audacity of an impudent scribbler of nonsense like Hegel was bold enough. And so it is tomfoolery of this sort which during the last fifty years has been spun out at great length under the name of cognitions of reason, and has filled hundreds of self-styled philosophical works. Such tomfoolery is also called, ironically one would imagine, science and scientific, even with this expression repeated ad nauseam. *Reason* (*Vernunft*), to which all such wisdom is so boldly and falsely imputed, is declared to be a "faculty of the supersensuous" as well as one "of ideas," in short, an oracular ability within us designed directly for *metaphysics.* But in the last fifty years there has been among the adepts a great difference of opinion about the way in which all these marvels and supersensuous apprehensions are perceived. According to the most audacious the faculty of reason has an immediate rational intuition of the Absolute, or even ad libitum of the infinite, and of the infinite's evolutions into the finite. According to others who are somewhat less pretentious, it is in the position of a hearer rather than of a seer, since it does not exactly perceive, but merely *hears and conceives* (*vernimmt*) what is happening in cloud-cuckoo-town [Tr.] [12] (from Aristophanes' *The Birds*). It then faithfully repeats this to the so-called understanding which thereupon writes philosophical compendiums. According to one of Jacobi's jests even the German for reason (*Vernunft*) is said to be derived from this so-called hearing and conceiving, as though it were not perfectly obvious that the German *Vernunft* is taken from language that is conditioned by reason, and from the hearing and conceiving (*Vernehmen*) of words, as distinct from mere sensuous hearing that animals have. But that wretched jest has flourished for half a century; it is regarded as a serious idea and even a proof, and has been repeated a thousand times. Finally, according to the least pretentious, the faculty of reason cannot see or hear and therefore receives neither the spectacle nor the account of all the aforesaid marvels. On the contrary, of these it has nothing but a mere presentiment (*Ahndung*);[13] but here the letter *d* is expunged from the word, whereupon *Ahnung* acquires its own peculiar touch of silliness. Backed by the sheepish looks of the apostle of such wisdom for the time being, this touch must of necessity secure admission for it.

My readers know that I accept the word *Idea* (*Idee*) only in its original Platonic sense, and that I have thoroughly discussed it especially in the third book of my chief work. The French and English, on the other hand, attach to the words *idée* or *idea* a very ordinary yet perfectly definite and distinct meaning. When, however, anyone speaks to the Germans about Ideas (*Ideen*), especially when the word is pronounced *Uedähen,* their heads begin to swim, all reflectiveness forsakes them, and they feel as if they were about to go up in a balloon. Here, then, there was something to do for our adepts of rational intuition; and so the most brazen of them all, the notorious charlatan Hegel, summarily called his principle of the world and of all things the Idea (*die Idee*), and here everyone really thought that he had something. If, however, we do not let ourselves be disconcerted but ask what the Ideas really are whose faculty is defined as that of reason (*Vernunft*), the explanation usually given is high-sounding, hollow, and confused verbiage. It is seen in involved periods of such length that, if the reader has not already fallen asleep in the middle, he finds himself at the end more in a state of stupefaction than in one of information gained; or indeed he even begins to suspect that something very much like chimeras might be intended. Meanwhile, if he wishes to become specially acquainted with such Ideas, all kinds of things are served up to him. Thus he may be offered the principal themes of scholasticism, which Kant himself unfortunately called Ideas of Reason, unjustifiably and erroneously, as I have shown in my criticism of his philosophy. But this he did merely to show them as something absolutely indemonstrable and theoretically groundless. And so these Ideas of Reason were the representations of God, of an immortal soul, and of a real objectively existing world and its order; as a variation, they are also cited merely as God, freedom, and immortality. Again, the reader may be served up with the Absolute with which we became acquainted in § 20 as the cosmological proof compelled to travel incognito. Sometimes it will be the infinite as opposed to the finite, for, as a rule, the German reader is quite content with this display of words, and does not see that ultimately the only clear thought he can get therefrom is "what has an end" and "what has no end." Moreover, "the Good, the True, and the Beautiful" are much in favour, especially with the sentimental and tender-hearted, as pretended Ideas, although they are simply three very wide and abstract concepts, in that they are drawn from innumerable things and relations, and are consequently very poor in substance, like a thousand other *abstracta* of a similar kind. As regards their content, I have shown in § 29 that truth is a quality belonging exclusively to judgements, and is thus a logical quality. As regards the other two *abstracta* here mentioned, I refer to the *World as Will and Representation*, Vol. I, § 65, and also to the whole of the third book of the same work. But if with these three meagre *abstracta* a really mysterious and pompous air is assumed and eyebrows are raised to the wig, young men might easily imagine there is something marvellous behind them, something quite peculiar and inexpressible, and that they thus merit the name of Ideas, and ought to be hitched to the triumphal car of that pretended metaphysical reason.

When, therefore, we are told that we possess a faculty for immediate material (i.e., furnishing the substance and not merely the form) supersensuous (i.e., transcending all possibility of experience) knowledge, a faculty expressly intended for metaphysical insight and dwelling within us for that purpose, and that our *faculty of reason* consists in this, then I must be so impolite as to call this a downright lie. For the least but honest self-examination must convince anyone that absolutely no such faculty exists within us. Moreover, in keeping with this, is the result obtained in the course of time from the investigations of qualified, competent, and honest thinkers, that what is inborn, and thus a priori and independent of experience, in the whole of our cognitive faculty is absolutely restricted to the *formal* part of knowledge, in other words, to the consciousness of the intellect's peculiar functions and of the manner of their only possible activity. But these functions, one and all, require material from without in order to furnish material knowledge. Thus there reside within us the forms of external objective intuitive perception as time and space; then the law of causality as a mere form of understanding by means of which this constructs the objective corporeal world; and finally the formal part of abstract knowledge. This is laid down and explained in *logic* which has therefore quite rightly been called by our ancestors the *theory of reason* (*Vernunftlehre*). This very logic, however, tells us also that *concepts* must expect to obtain their *material* and *content* from knowlege of *intuitive perception*; and judgements and conclusions, to which all the laws of logic refer, consist of concepts. In the same way the understanding, creating this knowledge of *intuitive perception*, takes from sensation the material that gives substance to its a priori forms.

Therefore all that is *material* in our knowledge, that is to say, all that cannot be reduced to subjective *form*, to a characteristic mode of activity, or to a function of the intellect, and consequently all the *material or substance* of our knowledge, comes from without, and thus ultimately from the objective intuitive perception of the corporeal world, such perception having its origin in sensation. Now it is this knowledge of intuitive perception, and, according to its material content, this empirical knowledge, which the faculty of *reason (Vernunft)*, *real* reason, then works up into concepts. These it sensuously fixes by means of words. In these it has the material for its endless combinations through judgements and syllogisms which constitute the web of our world of thought. *Reason (Vernunft)*, therefore, has absolutely no *material*, but only a *formal*, content which is the substance of logic; and so this contains mere forms and rules for the operations of thought. When it thinks, our faculty of reason is absolutely compelled to take its material from without, from the representations of intuitive perception which have been created by the understanding. This faculty of reason exercises its functions on those representations, since, when first forming *concepts*, it drops some of the different qualities of things and retains others, which are now combined into a concept. But the representations thereby forfeit their perceptibility; yet in return for this they become easier to survey and to handle, as I have already shown. And so this and this alone is the activity of the faculty of reason; on the other hand, it can never furnish *material from its own resources*. It has nothing but forms; it is feminine and merely conceives, but does not generate. It is no accident that reason is feminine in Germanic as well as Latin languages, whereas understanding is masculine.

When we say: "Sound reason teaches this," or "Reason should curb the passions" and other such expressions, we certainly do not mean that the faculty of reason furnishes material knowledge from its own resources. On the contrary, we point thereby to the results of rational reflection, and thus to logical inference from propositions which abstract knowledge, enriched by experience, has gradually gained, and by virtue of which we are able to have a clear and comprehensive survey not merely of what is empirically necessary and is therefore to be foreseen should the occasion arise, but also of the grounds and consequences of our own actions. "Rational" or "reasonable" is everywhere synonymous with "consistent" or "logical," as also conversely. Indeed logic is simply the natural method of the faculty of reason itself, expressed as a system of rules. Therefore those expressions (rational and logical) are related to each other as practice to theory. In precisely this sense we understand by a *rational* way of acting one that is entirely consistent, starts from general concepts, and is guided by abstract thoughts as resolutions; but not one that is determined by the fleeting impression of the moment. Yet nothing is decided thereby as regards the morality of such a course of action which may be good as well as bad. Detailed explanations of this are found in my "Criticism of the Kantian Philosophy," and also in the *Two Fundamental Problems of Ethics*, "Basis of Morality," Para. 6. Finally, knowledge from pure reason is that which has its origin in the *formal* part of our cognitive faculty, whether conceiving or perceiving, and consequently that which we can bring a priori to our consciousness, that is, without the help of experience. Such knowledge rests always on propositions of transcendental or even metalogical truth.

On the other hand, a faculty of reason furnishing material knowledge originally and from its own resources and thus giving us positive information beyond all possibility of experience, a faculty that would have to contain *innate Ideas* for this purpose, is a pure fiction of professors of philosophy, and a product of that dread created in them by Kant's *Critique of Pure Reason*. Do these gentlemen know a certain Locke, and have they read his works? Perhaps they did long ago, superficially and in places, and moreover in an inferior hack-translation, looking down on the great man with conscious superiority. For I have not yet observed that a knowledge of modern languages has increased in proportion to the deplorable decrease in that of the ancient. Of course they had no time to waste on such old fogies; indeed even a real and thorough knowledge of Kant's philosophy is to be found at best in a few, a very few, old heads. For the youth of the present generation of adults had to be devoted to the works of "Hegel's gigantic mind," of the "great Schleiermacher," and of the "sagacious and discerning Herbart." Alas! alas! the fatal thing about such university celebrities and about that praise for heros of the professor's chair, coming as it does from the lips of respectable collegues in office and of hopeful aspirants thereto, is precisely that mediocre minds—nature's mere manufactured articles—are extolled as great, as the exceptions and ornaments of mankind, and commended to honest and credulous youths devoid of judgement. These young men then devote all their youthful energies to the

sterile study of the endless and spiritless scribblings of such
men. They waste the short and valuable period allotted to
them for higher education instead of devoting it to real
instruction that is to be found in the works of rare and
genuine thinkers. These are the real exceptions among men,
"single swimmers in a waste of waves," [Tr.] [14] (Virgil,
Aeneid I, 118) who in the course of centuries have only now
and then come to the surface, just because nature made
only one of each kind and then "smashed the mould." [15]
For this generation they too would have been living minds,
had our young men not been cheated of their share by the
exceedingly pernicious praisers of the bad and those
members of the great band and brotherhood of mediocre
minds who always flourish and wave their banner as the
regular opponents of all that is great, genuine, and for them
humiliating. Through such men and their activities the age
has so declined that Kant's philosophy, which our fathers
understood only after years of serious study and strenuous
effort, has once more become something foreign to the
present generation. Thus it now stands before it "like an ass
listening to a lyre," [Tr.] [16] and attempts to attack it in a
coarse, crude, and blundering fashion, like barbarians who
throw stones at the statue of some Greek god that is foreign
to them. Since this is the case, it is now incumbent on me
to recommend Locke's first book as something new to the
champions of a reason that knows immediately, comprehends, and perceives, in short, of a reason that supplies
material knowledge from its own resources. Locke's work
has become world-famous in the last one hundred and fifty
years, and is expressly directed against all kinds of innate

knowledge. I specially recommend § § 21-26 of the third chapter. For although Locke goes too far in denying all innate truths, inasmuch as he extends his denial even to all formal knowledge, a point in which he was later most brilliantly corrected by Kant, he is nevertheless perfectly and undeniably right with regard to all material knowledge, i.e., knowledge that gives substance.

In my *Ethics* I have already stated what I must nevertheless repeat here because, as the Spanish proverb says: none so deaf as those who will not hear (*no hay peor sordo, que el que no quiere oír*); namely that if the faculty of *reason* were designed for metaphysics; if it were a faculty supplying the very substance and accordingly giving information beyond all possibility of experience, then on the subjects of metaphysics and thus also of religion, for they are the same thing, there would necessarily be among men just as much agreement as there is on the subjects of mathematics. Whoever differed from others in his views on such matters, would inevitably be regarded as not quite right in his head. But we have the very opposite, and on no theme is the human race so completely at variance as on the subject of metaphysics and religion. Ever since men have thought, complete systems of philosophy have everywhere been at variance, and some have been diametrically opposed to one another. Ever since men have believed (and this has been going on for an even longer time), religions have fought against one another with fire and sword, excommunications and cannon. But in times when faith was really lively and ardent, there were for sporadic dissenters not lunatic asylums, but the prisons of the Inquisition with all their paraphernalia. Thus experience here loudly and categorically contradicts the false assertion that reason is a faculty of direct metaphysical knowledge or, to speak more plainly, of inspirations from above. It is really high time that severe judgement was passed on such a faculty, for *horribile dictu*, so lame, so palpable a lie has been hawked round Germany for half a century. Year in year out it wanders from professor's chair to student's bench, and then back from bench to chair; indeed even among the French it has found a few simpletons who have allowed themselves to be taken in by the fairy tale which they now hawk round France. But the *bon sens* of the French will soon turn the *raison transcendentale* out of doors.

But where was the lie concocted and how did the fairy tale come into the world? I have to confess that unfortunately Kant's Practical Reason and its Categorical Imperative first gave rise to it. When once that practical reason had been accepted, nothing more was needed but the addition of a theoretical reason as its pendant or twin sister, a reason just as sovereign, and consequently proclaiming metaphysical truths *ex tripode*. I have described the brilliant success of the thing in the *Two Fundamental Problems of Ethics*, "Basis of Morality," Para. 6, to which I refer. Therefore, while admitting that Kant gave rise to this false assumption, I must nevertheless add that, whoever is fond of dancing readily finds a piper. It is indeed like a curse bearing heavily on the race of bipeds that, in virtue of their affinity for the absurd and bad, they are most easily pleased by the very worst, the very mistakes, even in the works of great minds, so that they praise and admire this part of their works, whereas the really admirable is allowed to pass almost unnoticed. At the present time exceedingly few are acquainted with what is truly great and really profound in Kant's philosophy; for when the serious study of his works ceased, their comprehension was also bound to come to an end. They are now read only cursorily for the purpose of historical information by those who imagine that after Kant something arrived, indeed something sound and solid. We therefore notice in all their talk about Kant's philosophy that they know only its husk or outer covering, have carried away only a rough sketch of it, have picked up a word here and there, but have never penetrated to the depths of its meaning and spirit. Now what such men have always liked best in Kant are first the Antinomies as something very strange, but then Practical Reason with its Categorical Imperative, and also Moral Theology that is based thereon. With this, however, Kant was never in earnest, for a theoretical dogma of exclusively practical value is like a wooden gun that can without risk be given to children; it really belongs also to the same category as "wash my skin but do not make it wet." But as regards the Categorical Imperative itself, Kant never asserted it as a fact; on the contrary, he repeatedly protested against it and served it up merely as the result of an extremely odd combination of concepts, just because he needed a sheet-anchor for morality. But the professors of philosophy have never gone to the bottom of the matter, so that prior to me it had apparently never been investigated. Instead of this, they hastened to bring the Categorical Imperative into repute as a firmly established fact under the purist name of "the Moral Law," which always reminds me of Bürger's *Mam'zelle Larègle*. In fact they have made of it something as massive as the stone Decalogue of Moses, and for them it must completely take the place thereof. Now in my essay "On the Basis of Morality," I have brought Practical Reason and its Categorical Imperative under the anatomical knife, and have so clearly and conclusively shown that there was never any life or truth in them, that I would like to see the man who could refute me with arguments and honestly help again on to its legs the Categorical Imperative. But this does not throw the professors of philosophy off their balance. They can no more dispense with their "Moral Law of Practical Reason" as a convenient *deux ex machina*[17] for establishing their morality than they can do without the freedom of the will; for they are two absolutely essential parts of their old woman's petticoat philosophy. Now it makes no difference that I have put to death these two, for so far as the professors are concerned, they are both still alive, just as a monarch already dead is sometimes permitted on political grounds to continue to reign for a few days. These gallant fellows simply use their old tactics towards my ruthless demolition of those two antiquated fictions. Silence, silence; they noiselessly slink past and behave as though nothing had happened, so that the public will imagine that whatever a man like me says is not worth listening to. Naturally; since they are qualified for philosophy by the ministry, whereas I am simply by nature. It is true that the ultimate result will be that these heroes act like that idealistically minded bird, the ostrich, which imagines that if only it covers its eyes, the hunter will no longer exist. Well now, all in good time; if only the public will rest content with the sterile twaddle, the insufferably tedious drawling of words, the arbitrary constructions of the Absolute, and the infant-school morality of these gentlemen—say till I am dead and they can then trim my works to their taste, then we shall see.

> The good and the true tomorrow
> May have its well-disposed friends,
> If only today the bad and base
> Still gain full favour and place.
> Goethe, *Der Westöstliche Diwan*, p. 97.

But do these gentlemen know what time of day it is? A long predicted epoch has set in; the Church is tottering, indeed so badly, that it is doubtful whether it will recover its centre of gravity; for faith has been lost. It is with the light of revelation as with other lights; some darkness is the condition. The number of those rendered unfit for belief by a certain degree and extent of knowledge has become considerable. This is testified by the general dissemination of that shallow rationalism which is showing ever more openly its bulldog face. It calmly sets to work to measure with its tailor's tape the profound mysteries of Christianity over which centuries have brooded and disputed, and in this respect it deems itself to be exceedingly clever. Above all it is the central dogma of Christianity, the doctrine of original sin, that has become for these shallow-brained rationalists the laughing-stock of children, just because for them nothing seems to be clearer or more certain than that the existence of everyone has begun with his birth, and that therefore he cannot possibly have come burdened with guilt into the world. How ingenious! And just as, when impoverishment and neglect gain the upper hand wolves begin to appear in villages, so does materialism, ever lying in wait, rear its head in these circumstances, and come forward hand in hand with its companion bestiality (called humanism by certain people). The need for knowledge grows with the inability to believe. There is a boiling-point on the scale of culture where all faith, revelation, and authorities evaporate; where man desires to judge for himself, and wishes to be not only instructed but also convinced. The leading-strings of childhood have fallen from him, and he wants to stand on his own feet. But here his metaphysical need (*World as Will and Representation*,Vol. II, Chap. 17) is just as ineradicable as is the physical. It is then that the desire for philosophy becomes serious, and mankind in its need summons all the thinkers it has ever produced. Hollow verbiage and the impotent efforts of intellectual eunuchs then no longer suffice. On the contrary, there is need for a philosophy seriously meant, in other words, one that is directed to truth and not to salaries and fees. Such a philosophy, therefore, does not ask whether it has to please ministers or councillors, or serve this or that religious cause for the time being. Rather does it show that the business of philosophy is quite different from that of providing a means of livelihood for the poor in spirit.

But I return to my theme. By means of an amplification needing a little audacity, a theoretical oracle was associated with the *practical* that Kant had falsely attributed to the faculty of reason (*Vernunft*). The honour of the invention is doubtless due to F. H. Jacobi, and from this gallant fellow the professors of philosophy gladly and gratefully accepted the precious gift; for they were thus helped out of the straits to which Kant had reduced them. That cold dispassionate reflective reason, which Kant had criticized so mercilessly, was degraded to the *understanding*, and henceforth had to bear that name; whereas the name reason was given to a wholly imaginary, false, and fictitious faculty. Here we had, so to speak, a little window that admitted us to the superlunal and even supernatural world. Through it we could receive, ready cut and dried, all the truths over which the former old-fashioned, honest, and reflective reason had for centuries vainly contended and exhausted itself. And German so-called philosophy has for the last fifty years been based on such a wholly false and fabricated faculty; first as the free construction and projection of the absolute *ego* and its emanations into the *non-ego*; then as the intellectual intuition of the absolute identity or indifference, and of its evolutions into nature; or again as the origin of God from his own dark ground or groundlessness, *à la* Jacob Boehme; finally as the pure self-thinking of the absolute Idea, the ballet scene of self-moving concepts. In addition to all this, there is still the immediate apprehension of the Divine, the supersensuous, the Deity, verity, beauty, and of as many other "-ties" as may be desired, or even the mere presentiment (*Ahnen* without the *d*) of all these marvels. And so this is reason, is it? Oh no; it is a farce which shall serve as a last resource for professors of philosophy who are embarrassed by Kant's serious Critiques so that somehow, *per fas aut nefas,* [18] they can palm off as the results of philosophy the subjects of

181

their country's established religion.

Thus the first duty of all professorial philosophy is to establish on a philosophical basis and to settle beyond all doubt the doctrine of God, creator and ruler of the world, a personal and therefore an individual being endowed with understanding and will, who has produced the world out of nothing and rules it with the highest wisdom, power, and goodness. But with regard to serious philosophy, the professors are thus put into an awkward position. Kant came, the *Critique of Pure Reason* was written more than sixty years ago, and the result was that all proofs of the existence of God, furnished during Christian centuries and reducible to the only three possible methods of demonstration, are quite unable to achieve what is required. Indeed the impossibility of every such proof and with it that of all speculative theology are fully demonstrated a priori; and naturally this is not done in a manner that in our day has become fashionable, namely with hollow verbiage or Hegelian twaddle, whereof anyone can make just what he likes. On the contrary, it is done quite seriously and honestly in the good old-fashioned way so that for sixty years, however awkward the matter may have been for many, no one has been able to raise any serious objection to Kant's argument; indeed in consequence thereof the proofs of the existence of God are wholly discredited and no longer in use. In fact the professors of philosophy have since turned up their noses at them, and even show a decided contempt for them, because, as they say, the thing is so self-evident that it is ridiculous to try to demonstrate it. Indeed! If only this had been known earlier! For centuries men would not have worn themselves out looking for such proofs, and it would not have been necessary for Kant to crush them with the whole weight of his *Critique of Reason.* With the above-mentioned contempt many will, of course, be reminded of the fox and the sour grapes. Moreover, if anyone would like to see a short specimen of it, he will find a really characteristic one in Schelling's *Philosophische Schriften* (Vol. I, 1809, p. 152). Now while others were consoling themselves with Kant's assertion that it was also impossible to prove the nonexistence of God, as though the old rascal did·not know that *affirmanti incumbit probatio,*[19] Jacobi's admirable invention came to the rescue of our perplexed professors, and conferred on the German savants of this century a quite peculiar faculty of reason that had never been previously known or heard of.

However, all these tricks and dodges were quite unnecessary. For the impossibility to prove the existence of God does not in the least call in question that existence itself, for it stands unshakable on much firmer ground. Indeed it is a matter of revelation, and of course this is the more certain, as it was vouchsafed solely and exclusively to those who for that reason are called the chosen race. This is evident from the fact that the knowledge of God, as the personal ruler and creator of the world who made everything well, is found simply and solely in the religious doctrine of the Jews and in the two faiths derived therefrom which in the wider sense might be called Jewish sects. But the knowledge of God is not found in the religion of any other race, ancient or modern. For it will surely never occur to anyone to confuse Almighty God with, say, the *Brahma* of the Hindus, who lives and suffers in you and me, in my horse and in your dog, or even in Brahma who is born and dies to make way for other Brahmas, and whose production of the world is regarded as sin and guilt,[20] least of all with beguiled Saturn's voluptuous son whom Prometheus defies and whose fall he prophesies. But if we examine *that* religion which has the greatest number of followers on earth and thus the majority of mankind in its favour, and which in this respect can be regarded as foremost, namely Buddhism we can now no longer disguise the fact that it is just as decidedly and expressly atheistic as it is strictly idealistic and ascetic. In fact it is atheistic to the extent that, when the doctrine of pure theism is brought to the notice of its priests, they expressly reject it out of hand. Thus in an article handed to a Catholic bishop by the high priest of the Buddhists at Ava (as reported in the *Asiatic Researches*, Vol. VI, p. 268, and also in Sangermano's *Description of the Burmese Empire*, p. 81), he reckoned as one of the six damnable heresies the doctrine "that a being exists who created the world and all things, and who alone is worthy of worship." (See I. J. Schmidt's *Forschungen im Gebiete der ältern Bildungsgeschichte Mittelasiens*, St. Petersburg, 1824, p. 276.) For this very reason, I. J. Schmidt of St. Petersburg, a first rate scholar who in my opinion is undoubtedly the greatest European expert on Buddhism, says in his work *Über die Verwandtschaft der gnostischen Lehren mit dem Buddhaismus*, p. 9: "In the writings of the Buddhists we cannot find any positive hint or suggestion of a supreme being as the principle of creation, and it seems that, whenever this

subject crops up in the course of argument, it is intentionally avoided." In his *Forschungen im Gebiete der ältern
Bildungsgeschichte Mittelasiens*, p. 180 he says: "The
system of Buddhism knows of no eternal, uncreated, single,
divine being who existed before all time and created
everything visible and invisible. This idea is quite foreign to
it, and in Buddhist books we do not find the slightest trace
thereof. There is just as little mention of a creation; it is
true that the visible universe is not without beginning, but
it *originated* out of empty space in accordance with
consistent, immutable, natural laws. But we should be
mistaken in assuming that something—call it fate or
nature—were regarded or revered by the Buddhists as a
divine principle. On the contrary, it is precisely this
development of empty space, this precipitate therefrom, or
this division into innumerable parts, this matter that has
now arisen, which is the evil of *Jirtintshi*, or of the universe
in its inner and outer relations from which *Oktshilang* or
continuous change according to immutable laws has *originated*, after those laws were established by that evil."
Again, in his lecture given at the St. Petersburg Academy on
15 September 1830, p. 26, he says: "The expression
creation is foreign to Buddhism, since it knows only of
world origins or formations"; and p. 27: "It must be seen
that with their system there cannot be any idea of an
original, divine creation." A hundred such examples could
be quoted. But I wish to draw attention to yet another,
because it is quite popular and indeed official. Thus the
third volume of that very instructive Buddhist work
Mahāvamsa, Raja-ratnacari and Raja-vali, from the Singha-

lese, by E. Upham, London, 1833, contains the official interrogatories, translated from Dutch reports, which the Dutch governor of Ceylon conducted with the high-priests of the five principal pagodas separately and successively about the year 1766. The contrast between the interlocutors who cannot really reach an agreement is highly entertaining. Imbued with love and compassion for all living beings in accordance with the teachings of their religion, even if such beings should be Dutch governors, the priests show the greatest willingness in their efforts to give satisfactory answers to the governor's questions. But the naïve, sincere, and artless atheism of these pious and even encratistic high-priests conflicts with the deep convictions of the governor who even in his cradle had been infected with Judaism. His faith has become second nature to him and he cannot possibly see that these priests are not theists. Therefore he always asks afresh about the supreme being who created the world and other such questions. But they are of the opinion that there cannot be any higher being than the triumphant Perfect One, the Buddha Shakia Muni who, though born a king's son, voluntarily lived as a mendicant, and to the end of his days preached his sublime teaching for the redemption of mankind in order to save us all from the misery of constant rebirth. They are of the opinion that the world is not made by anyone;[*] that it is self-created; and that nature spreads it out and draws it in again. They say that it is that, which existing, does not exist; that it is the necessary accompaniment of rebirths; but that these are the consequences of our sinful conduct, and so on. And so these discourses continue for a

186

hundred pages. I mention such facts mainly because it is positively scandalous how, even today in the works of German scholars, religion and theism are usually regarded without more ado as identical and synonymous; whereas religion is related to theism as the genus to a single species. In fact only Judaism and theism are identical. Therefore all races who are not Jews, Christians, or Mohammedans are stigmatized by us with the common name of heathen. Because of the doctrine of the Trinity even Christians are reproached by Mohammedans and Jews with not being pure theists. For whatever anyone may say Christianity has Indian blood in its veins, and thus has a constant tendency to be rid of Judaism. Kant's *Critique of Pure Reason* is the most serious attack ever made on theism, and this is why the professors of philosophy have hastened to put his work on the shelf. If it had appeared in Buddhist countries, then in accordance with the above quotations one would have seen in it nothing but an edifying treatise on the more thorough refutation of its heretics, and the more salutary confirmation of the orthodox doctrine of idealism, namely that of the merely apparent existence of this world that is presented to our senses. Even the other two religions existing with Buddhism in China, those of Lao-tze and Confucius, are just as atheistic. This is precisely why the missionaries were unable to translate into Chinese the first verse of the Pentateuch, because that language has no expressions for God and creation. Even the missionary Gützlaff has the honesty to say on page 18 of his recently published *Geschichte des chinesischen Reichs*: "It is extraordinary that none of the philosophers (in China), who nevertheless possessed the light of nature in full measure, has risen to knowledge of a creator and lord of the universe." Wholly in accord with this is what I. F. Davis (*The Chinese*, Chap. XV, p. 156) quotes; thus Milne, the translator of the *Shing-yu*, says in the preface to this work how it can be seen "that the bare light of nature, as it is called, even when aided by all the light of pagan philosophy, is totally incapable of leading men to the knowledge and worship of the true God." All this confirms the fact that revelation is the sole foundation of theism, as it must be, if revelation is not to be superfluous. Incidentally, it should be observed that the word atheism contains a surreptitious assumption, in that it assumes in advance that theism is self-evident. Instead, one should say non-Judaism and non-Jew instead of atheist; this would be the more honest course.

Now since, as I have said, the existence of God is a matter of revelation and is firmly established thereby, it needs no human verification. But philosophy is really only the idle and superfluous attempt to leave reason, thus man's ability to think, deliberate, and reflect, entirely to its own devices for once, just as a child on a lawn occasionally has its leading-strings removed and is allowed to try its strength, to see what the result will be. Such tests and attempts are called speculation, and here it is in the nature of the case that it should for once set aside and ignore all authority, both human and divine, and go its own way in search of the highest and most important truths. If on this basis the result of speculation is none other than that, previously mentioned, of our great Kant, then it should not on that account at once renounce all honesty and conscientiousness, and follow secret paths like a rogue in order to get back in some way on to the ground and basis of Judaism as its *conditio sine qua non.*[21] On the contrary, it should now go simply and honestly in search of truth on other paths that may be opened up to it; but it should never follow any other light than that of reason. It should pursue its course calmly and confidently, unconcerned about where this may lead, like a man working at his daily vocation.

If our professors of philosophy understand the matter in a different light, and imagine that they cannot honestly eat their bread as long as they have not set Almighty God on his throne (as though he were in need of them), then this explains why they cannot relish my writings and I am certainly not their man. For of course I cannot deal in matters of this kind, nor do I have to bring, at every fair as they do, the latest reports of the Almighty.

1. "Statement concerning all and none," attributed to Aristotle. Whatever is affirmed (or denied) of an entire class or kind may be affirmed (or denied) of any part. [Tr.]
2. Ἄνευ μὲν γὰρ τῶν καθόλου οὐκ ἔστιν ἐπιστήμην λαβεῖν (absque universalibus enim non datur scientia).
3. "Between a dog and a wolf." [Tr.]
4. Whoever regards this as an exaggeration should consider the fate of Goethe's theory of colour; and if he is surprised at my finding therein evidence of this, he himself has furnished a second proof of my point.
5. "Which are too good for words." [Tr.]
6. Οὐδέποτε νοεῖ ἄνευ φαντάσματος ἡ ψυχή (anima sine phantasmate nunquam intelligit) . . . ὅταν θεωρῇ, ἀνάγκη ἅμα φάντασμά τι θεωρεῖν (qui contemplatur, necesse est, una cum phantasmate contempletur) . . . νοεῖν οὐκ ἔστιν- ἄνευ φαντάσματος (fieri non potest, ut sine phantasmate quid quam intelligatur).
7. Necesse est, eum, qui ratiocinatur et intelligit, phantasmata speculari; . . . Oportet intelligentem phantasmata speculari. . . . Dicit Aristotles: oportet scire volentem, phantasmata speculari.
8. Κατ' ἐξοχήν.
9. Quia Logicae suscepi patrocinium, Metalogicus insriptus est liber.
10. Quae docendo, discendo, communicando, disceptando, judicando, conciliat inter se homines. . . . Rationem dico, et, si placet, pluribus verbis, mentem, consilium, cogitationem, prudentiam. . . . Ratio, qua una praestamis belius, per quam conjectura valemus, argumentamur, refellimus, disserimus, conficimus aliquid, concludimus.
11. "To the greater glory of God." [Tr.]
12. Νεφελοκοκκυγία.
13. An old spelling of the modern Ahnung. [Tr.]
14. Rari nantes in gurgite vasto.
15. Cf. Ariosto, X, 84. [Tr.]
16. Ὄνος πρὸς λύραν.
17. "A god from the [theatrical] machine." [Tr.]

18. "By hook or by crook." [Tr.]

19. "The proof is incumbent on him who affirms anything."
[Tr.]

20. "If Brahma be unceasingly employed in the creation of
worlds, . . . how can tranquility be obtained by inferior or-
ders of being?" *Prabodha Chandro Daya,* translated by J.
Taylor, p. 23. Brahma is also part of the Trimurti, but this
is the personification of nature, as generation, perservation,
and death. He therefore represents the first of these.

*Κόσμον τόνδε, φησὶν Ἡράκλειτος, οὔτε τις θεῶν οὔτ'ανθρώ-
πων ἐποίησεν. ["Neither a god nor a human being has made
this world, says Heraclitus." Plutarch, *De animae procreati-
one,* c. 5. Tr.]

21. "Absolutely necessary condition." [Tr.]

CHAPTER VI

ON THE THIRD CLASS OF OBJECTS FOR THE SUBJECT AND THE FORM OF THE PRINCIPLE OF SUFFICIENT REASON RULING THEREIN

§ 35. Explanation of This Class of Objects

The formal part of complete representations, namely the intuitive perceptions, given a priori, of the forms of the outer and inner senses, i.e., of space and time, constitute the third class of objects for the faculty of representation.

As pure intuitions, they are objects of that faculty by themselves and apart from the complete representations and from the determinations of being full or empty, which are first added by these representations. For even mere points and lines cannot possibly be depicted on paper, but can be intuitively perceived only a priori, just as the infinite extension and divisibility of space and time are objects of pure intuition alone and are foreign to empirical intuitive perception. What distinguishes this class of representations, in which time and space are *pure intuitions*, from the first, in which they are *sensuously perceived* (and moreover conjointly), is matter. I have therefore declared matter to be the perceptibility of time and space, on the one hand, and causality that has become objective, on the other.

The understanding's form of causality, however, is not separately and by itself an object of the faculty of representation, but enters our consciousness only with and in the material part of our knowledge.

§ 36. Principle of Sufficient Reason and Being

Space and time are so constituted that all their parts stand in mutual relation and, on the strength of this, every part is determined and conditioned by another. In space this relation is called *position*, in time *succession*. These relations are peculiar and differ entirely from all other possible relations of our representations. Therefore neither the understanding nor the faculty of reason by means of mere concepts is capable of grasping them, but they are made intelligible to us simply and solely by means of pure intuition a priori. For it is impossible to explain clearly from mere concepts what are above and below, right and left, front and back, before and after. Kant quite rightly confirms this by saying that the difference between the right and left gloves cannot possibly be made intelligible except by means of intuition. Now the law whereby the parts of space and time determine one another as regards those relations is what I call the *principle of sufficient reason of being, principium rationis sufficientis essendi.* An example of this relation is already given in § 15 in the connexion between the sides and angles of a triangle. There it is shown that this relation is quite different from that between cause and effect and also from that between ground of knowledge and consequent; and so the condition may here be called ground or reason of *being, ratio essendi*. It is evident that insight into such a *ground of being* may become a ground of knowledge, just as insight into the law of causality and its application to a definite case is the ground of knowledge of the effect; but this in no way abolishes the complete difference between ground of being, ground of becoming, and ground of knowing. In many cases what is *consequence* according to *one* form of our principle is ground according to another; thus the effect is very often the ground of knowledge of the cause. For example, the rising of the mercury in the thermometer is the *consequence* of increased heat according to the law of causality; whereas according to the principle of sufficient reason or ground of knowing it is the *ground of reason*, the ground of knowing the increased heat, as well as of the judgement that states this.

§ 37. Ground or Reason of Being in Space

In space the position of each of its parts, say of a given line (the same holds good of areas, bodies, and points) relative to any other line, also determines absolutely its position (totally different from the first) relative to every other possible line; so that the latter position is to the former in the relation of consequent to ground. As the position of the line relative to any position of other possible lines likewise determines its position relative to all others, and thus the position just now assumed as determined relative to the first, it is immaterial which we consider first as the determined and the determinant of the others, that is to say, which we will regard as *ratio*, and which others as *rationata*. This is because there is no succession in space, for it is precisely through the union of space with time, to form the complete and general representation of the complex of experience, that the representation of coexistence arises. Thus with the ground or reason of being in space there prevails everywhere an analogue to so-called reciprocity or reciprocal effect. In § 48 I discuss this more fully when considering the reciprocity of grounds or reasons. Now since as regards its position every line is determined by all others just as much as it determines them, it is a matter of indifference whether we consider any line merely as determinant of others and not as determined, and the position of each relative to any other admits the question of its position relative to a third, and by virtue of this second position, the first necessarily is as it is. Therefore it is absolutely impossible to find an end *a parte ante*[1] in the concatenation of the grounds or reasons of being or in that of the grounds or reasons of becoming, and, because of the infinity of space and of the lines possible therein, it is also impossible to discover an end *a parte post.*[1] All possible relative spaces are figures because they are bounded and limited, and, on account of the common boundaries, all these figures have their ground

196

or reason of being in one another. The *series rationum essendi*[2] in space, like the *series rationum fiendi,*[3] continues therefore ad infinitum, and indeed not only in one direction, like the latter, but in all.

A proof of all this is impossible; for these are propositions whose truth is transcendental, since they have their ground directly in the intuition of space that is given to us a priori.

§ 38. Ground or Reason of Being in Time. Arithmetic

In time every moment is conditioned by the previous one. Here the ground or reason of being, as the law of succession, is so simple because time has only one dimension; consequently in it there cannot be any diversity or multiplicity of relations. Every moment is conditioned by the previous one; only through that predecessor can this moment be reached. It is only insofar as that other was and has elapsed. All counting depends on this nexus of the parts of time, and its words serve merely to mark the single stages of succession; consequently, the whole of arithmetic depends on it, a science that teaches absolutely nothing but methodical abbreviations of counting. Each number presupposes the preceding numbers as the grounds or reasons of its being; I can reach ten only by going through all the preceding numbers; and only by virtue of this insight into the ground of being, do I know that where there are ten, so are there eight, six, four.

It is only insofar as the other was

197

§ 39. Geometry

The whole of geometry also rests on the nexus of the position of the parts of space. It would thus be an insight into that nexus; but, as I have said, as such an insight is not possible through mere concepts, but only through intuition, every geometrical proposition would have to be reduced to this, and the proof would consist merely in our clearly bringing out the nexus whose intuition is required; more we could not do. We find, however, that the treatment of geometry is quite different. Only Euclid's twelve axioms are allowed to rest on mere intuition, and of these only the ninth, eleventh, and twelfth, properly speaking, rest on separate, different intuitions. All the others, however, rest on the view that in science we are not concerned, as in experience, with real things existing by themselves side by side and capable of infinite variety, but rather with concepts, and in mathematics with *normal intuitions*, that is, with figures and numbers, which legislate for all experience and thus combine the comprehensiveness of the concept with the complete definiteness of individual representations. For although, as representations of intuitive perception, they are determined throughout with precision, and in *this* way leave no room for universality through what is left undetermined, they are nevertheless universal because they are the mere forms of all phenomena, and as such hold good of all real objects to which such a form belongs. Therefore what Plato says of his Ideas would hold good of these normal intuitions, even in geometry, as well as of concepts, namely that two cannot exist exactly alike because such would be only one.[4] I say that this would hold good also of normal intuitions in geometry if it were not that, as exclusively *spatial* objects, they differ through mere juxtaposition and hence through *place*. According to Aristotle, Plato himself made this remark: "Further he asserts that, in comparison with the things of the senses and with the Ideas, the creations of mathematics hold the mean, insofar as they differ from things of the senses by being eternal and immovable, but from the Ideas by being many and equal, whereas each of the Ideas exists only as a unity." [Tr.][5] (*Metaphysics*, I, 6 which should be compared with X, 1.) Now the mere view that such a difference of place does not abolish the rest of the identity seems to me to be capable of replacing those nine axioms, and of being more suitable to the true nature of science whose purpose is to know the particular from the general, than is the statement of nine different axioms that are all based on one view. Thus what Aristotle says, (*Metaphysics*, X, 3) "with these equality constitutes unity," [Tr.][6] will then apply to geometrical figures.

Yet no such distinction of juxtaposition holds good of normal intuitions in time, of numbers, but simply the *identitas indiscernibilium*,[7] Leibniz's principle according to which two things not discernible are identical, as of concepts; and we have only one five and one seven. Here too may be the reason why $7 + 5 = 12$ is a synthetical proposition a priori, resting on pure intuition as Kant profoundly discovered, and not an identical proposition, as Herder imagines in his *Metakritik*. $12 = 12$ is an identical proposition. Thus in geometry it is only with the axioms that we appeal to intuition. All the other theorems are demonstrated, that is to say, a ground or reason of knowledge of the theorem is stated, which forces everyone to assume that the theorem is true. Hence the logical, not the transcendental, truth of the theorem is demonstrated (§ § 30 and 32); and as this lies in the ground of being and not in that of knowing, it never becomes evident except by means of intuition. This explains why, after such a geometrical demonstration, we certainly are convinced that the demonstrated proposition is true, but we by no means see why what is stated by the proposition is as it is. In other words, we do not have the ground or reason of being, but the desire for it has by now usually arisen. For proof by showing the ground of knowledge produces only conviction (*convictio*), not insight (*cognitio*). Therefore it might possibly be more correctly called *elenchus*[8] than *demonstratio*. This is why it usually leaves behind an uncomfortable feeling, such as is everywhere given by an observed want of insight; and here the want of knowledge *why* a thing is as it is makes itself felt through the given certainty *that* it is as it is. The feeling is similar to that which we have when something has been conjured into or out of our pocket, and we cannot conceive how this was done. The ground of knowledge, given without that of being, as is done in such demonstrations, is analogous to many theories in physics. These present the phenomenon without being able to state the cause, as for instance, Leidenfrost's experiment insofar as it also succeeds in a platinum crucible. On the other hand, the ground of being of a geometrical proposition recognized by intuition gives satisfaction, as does all acquired knowledge. When we have the ground of being, our conviction of the truth of the proposition is based solely thereon, and certainly no longer on that of knowledge which is given by demonstration. Take, for example, the sixth proposition of the first book of Euclid: "If in a triangle two angles are equal, the sides subtending them are also equal." Euclid's demonstration is as follows (see Fig. 3):

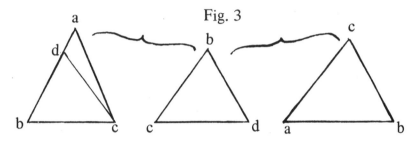

Fig. 3

Let *abc* be a triangle having the angle *abc* equal to the angle *acb*, then the side *ac* is equal to the side *ab*.

For if *ac* is not equal to *ab*, then one of them is greater than the other. Let *ab* be greater; from *ba* cut off *bd* equal to *ac*, and draw *dc*. Now since (in the triangles *dbc, abc*) *db* equals *ac*, and *bc* is common to both, the two sides *db* and *bc* are equal to the two sides *ac* and *cb*, each taken separately, and the angle *dbc* is equal to the angle *acb*, and the base *dc* is equal to the base *ab*, and the triangle *abc* is equal to the triangle *dcb*, the greater is equal to the smaller, which is absurd. Therefore *ab* is not unequal to *ac*, consequently *ab* is equal to *ac*.

In this proof we now have a ground of knowledge of the truth of the theorem. But who bases his conviction of that geometrical truth on this proof? On the contrary, we base our conviction on the ground of being that is known through intuitive perception. If by virtue of this ground (through a necessity that cannot be further demonstrated but only intuitively perceived) from the two ends of a line two others are drawn equally inclined to each other, they can meet only at a point equidistant from these two ends. For the two angles that arise are really only one, which appears as two merely because of the opposite position; and so there is no reason why the lines should meet at any point nearer to the one end than to the other.

Through knowledge of the ground of being we see the necessary inference of the conditioned from its condition, here the equality of the sides from that of the angles, in other words, their connexion; but through the ground of knowledge we see only the coexistence of the two. Indeed it might even be maintained that the usual method of proofs merely convinces us of the coexistence of the two in the actual figure given as an example, but certainly not of their permanent coexistence. For as the necessary connexion is not shown, the conviction we acquire of this truth is based merely on induction, and rests on the fact that we so find it in every figure we make. Of course, it is only in such simple theorems as Euclid's sixth that the ground of being is so evident; yet I am convinced that with every theorem, even the most complicated, it must be possible to demonstrate it, and to reduce the certainty of the proposition to such a simple intuition. Moreover, everyone is just as a priori conscious of the necessity of such a ground of being for every spatial relation as he is of the necessity of the cause for every change. Naturally in complicated theorems it is bound to be very difficult to state the ground of being. Therefore simply to make my meaning somewhat clearer, I will now try to reduce to its ground of being a slightly more complicated proposition in which, however, that ground is at any rate not immediately obvious. I pass by ten theorems and come to the sixteenth. "In every triangle in which one side has been produced, the exterior angle is greater than either of the two interior opposite angles." Euclid's proof is as follows (see Fig. 4):

Let *abc* be a triangle; produce *bc* to *d*; then the exterior angle *acd* is greater than either of the interior opposite angles. ... Bisect the side *ac* at *e* and join *be* and produce *be* to *z* making *ez* equal

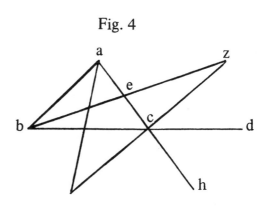

Fig. 4

to *eb*. Join *zc* and produce *ac* to *h*. Now as *ae* equals *ec* and *be* equals *ez*, the two sides *ae* and *eb* are equal to the two sides *ce* and *ez*, each taken separately, and the angle *aeb* is equal to the angle *zec* for they are vertical and opposite angles. Therefore the base *ab* equals the base *zc*, and the triangle *abe* is equal to the triangle *zec*, and the remaining angles of one triangle to the remaining angles of the other, consequently the angle *bae* to the angle *ecz*. But *ecd* is greater than *ecz*, consequently the angle *acd* is also greater than the angle *bae*. Also if *bc* is bisected, it can be proved in a similar way that the angle *bch*, i.e., its vertical and opposite angle *acd* is also greater than *abc*.

My proof of the same proposition would be as follows (see Fig. 5):

For the angle *bac* to be even equal to, let alone greater than, the angle *acd*, the line *ba* on to *ca* would have to lie in the same direction as *bd* (for this is pre-

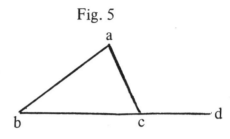

Fig. 5

cisely what is meant by equality of the angles), in other words, it would have to be parallel to *bd*, that is to say, *ba* and *bd* must never meet. But to form a triangle they must meet (ground of being), and thus do the opposite of what would be required for the angle *bac* merely to be equal to the angle *acd*.

For the angle *abc* to be even equal to, let alone greater than, the angle *acd* the line *ba* must lie in the same direction onto *bd* as does *ac* (for this is precisely what is meant by equality of the angles), that is to say, it must be parallel to *ac*, in other words, *ba* and *ac* must never meet. But in order to form a triangle they must meet and thus do the opposite of what would be required for the angle *abc* merely to be equal to the angle *acd*.

With all this I have certainly not suggested a new method of mathematical demonstrations, or tried to substitute my proof for Euclid's to which it is unsuited by reason of its whole nature, and because it already presupposes the conception of parallel lines, which comes only later in Euclid. I have endeavoured merely to show what the ground of being is, and how it differs from the ground of knowledge, since ground of knowledge produces only *convictio* which is something quite different from insight into the ground of being. Geometry aims only at producing *convictio* which, as I have said, gives rise to an uncomfortable impression, but affords no insight into the ground of being, whereas this, like all insight, is satisfactory and gratifying. This fact and others might be the reason why many otherwise eminent minds dislike mathematics.

Fig. 6

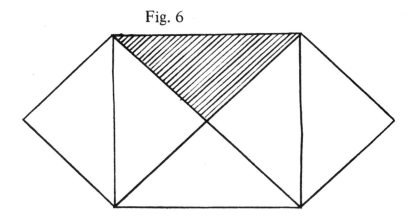

I cannot refrain from again giving Figure 6, although it has already been given elsewhere.[9] The mere sight of it without any words conveys twenty times more conviction of the truth of the Pythagorean theorem than does Euclid's mousetrap proof. The reader who is interested in this chapter will find its subject further discussed in the *World as Will and Representation* (Vol. I, § 15, and Vol. II, Chap. 13).

Footnotes

1. *A parte ante*, from the side of the before, referring to duration previous to a given event or point. *A parte post*, from the side of the after, referring to duration subsequent to a given event or point. [Tr.]
2. "The series of grounds or reasons of being." [Tr.]
3. "The series of grounds or reasons of becoming." [Tr.]
4. The *Platonic Ideas* may perhaps be described as normal intuitions which would be valid, like the mathematical, not only for the formal, but also for the material, part of complete representations. Hence they may be described as complete representations which, as such, would be determined throughout, and yet, like concepts, would at the same time concern many things, in other words, as representatives of concepts which, however, would be quite adequate to them, according to my explanation in § 28.
5. Ἔτι δὲ παρὰ τὰ αἰσθητὰ καὶ τὰ εἴδη, τὰ μαθηματικὰ τῶν πραγμάτων εἶναί φησι μεταξύ, διαφέροντα τῶν μὲν αἰσθητῶν τῷ ἀΐδια καὶ ἀκίνητα εἶναι τῶν δὲ εἰδῶν τῷ τὰ μὲν πόλλ' ἄττα ὅμοια εἶναι, τὸ δὲ εἶδος αὐτὸ ἕν ἕκαστον μόνον (*item praeter sensibilia et species, mathematica rerum ait media esse, a sensibilibus quidem differentia eo, quod perpetua et immobilia sunt, a speciebus vero eo, quod illorum quidem multa quaedam similia sunt, species vero ipsa unaquaeque sola*).
6. Ἐν τούτοις· ἡ ἰσότης ἑνότης (*in illis aequalitas unitas est*).
7. "Identity of indiscernibles." [Tr.]
8. A syllogism that establishes the contradictory of a proposition attacked; a refutation. [Tr.]
9. *The World as Will and Representation*, Vol. I, § 15.

CHAPTER VII

ON THE FOURTH CLASS OF OBJECTS FOR THE SUBJECT AND THE FORM OF THE PRINCIPLE OF SUFFICIENT REASON RULING THEREIN

§ 40. General Explanation

The last class of objects for the faculty of representation which is still to be considered is one that is quite special but very important. For each individual it comprises only *one* object, the immediate object of the inner sense, *the subject of willing,* which is object for the knowing subject, and indeed is given only to the inner sense. Hence it appears only in time not in space, and even in time with an important limitation, as we shall see.

§ 41. Subject of Knowing and Object

All knowledge inevitably presupposes subject and object; and so even self-consciousness is not absolutely simple, but, like our consciousness of other things (i.e., the faculty of intuitive perception), is divided into a known and

Arthur Schopenhauer

a knower. Now here the known appears absolutely and exclusively as will.

Accordingly, the subject knows itself only as a *willer*, not as a *knower*. For the ego that represents, thus the subject of knowing, can itself never become representation or object, since, as the necessary correlative of all representations, it is their condition. On the contrary, the fine passage from the sacred *Upanishad* applies: "It is not to be seen: it sees everything; it is not to be heard: it hears everything; it is not to be known: it knows everything; and it is not to be recognized: it recognizes everything. Besides this seeing, knowing, hearing, and recognizing entity there is no other." [Tr.]¹ (*Oupnekhat*, Vol. I, p. 202. Cf. *Brihadaranyaka Upanishad*, III, 7, 23.)

Consequently, there is no *knowledge of knowing*, since this would require that the subject separated itself from knowing and yet knew that knowing; and this is impossible.

My answer to the objection: "I not only know, but know also that I know," would be: "Your knowing that you know differs from your knowing only in the expression. 'I know that I know' states nothing more than 'I know', and this again, without further qualification, says nothing more than 'I' or 'ego'. If your knowing and your knowledge of this knowing are two different things, then just try to have each separately and by itself, thus first of all to know without being aware of this, and then again to know merely about knowing without this knowledge being at the same time knowing. We may, of course, abstract from all special knowing, and arrive at the proposition 'I know', which for us is the last possible abstraction, but

208

which is identical with the proposition 'objects exist for me', and this in turn is identical with 'I am subject', which contains nothing but the simple word 'I'."

But then it might be asked how the subject's various powers of knowledge, sensibility, understanding, and faculty of reason, are known to us, if the subject is not known. These are not known to us through knowing having become for us an object, otherwise there would not be so many contradictory judgements about them. On the contrary, they are inferred; or more correctly they are universal expressions of the established classes of representations, which are at all times more or less definitely distinguished in those very powers of knowledge. But with regard to the necessary correlative of those representations as their condition, namely to the subject, those powers are abstracted from the representations. Consequently, they are related to the classes of representations precisely as the subject in general is to the object in general. Now with the subject the object is also at once assumed (for even the word would otherwise be without meaning), and in the same way the subject is at once assumed with the object. Hence being subject means exactly the same as having an object, and being object means just the same as being known by the subject. In precisely the same manner, with an object *determined in any way*, the subject also is at once assumed as *knowing in just such a way*. To this extent it is immaterial whether I say that objects have such and such special and inherent determinations, or that the subject knows in such and such ways. It is immaterial whether I say that objects are divisible into such and such classes, or that such and such different powers of knowledge are peculiar to the subject. Traces even of this insight are to be found in Aristotle, that strange mixture of profundity and superficiality; in general the seeds of critical philosophy are to be found in his works. In *De anima*, III, 8, he says: "In a certain sense the mind is all that exists." [Tr.] [2] Again: 'O νοῦς ἔστιν εἶδος εἴδων, in other words, the understanding is the form of forms, καὶ ἡ αἴσθησις εἶδος αἰσθητῶν, and sensibility the form of objects of the senses. Accordingly, it is all one whether we say "sensibility and understanding are no more," or "the world is at an end." It is immaterial whether we say "there are no concepts," or "the faculty of reason has gone and only animals remain."

Failure to recognize this relation gave rise to the controversy between realism and idealism, appearing ultimately as the dispute of the old dogmatism with the Kantians, or of ontology and metaphysics with the transcendental aesthetic and transcendental logic. This dispute is due to the failure to see that relation with reference to the first and third classes of representations which were established by me, just as in the Middle Ages the dispute between Realists and Nominalists resulted from a failure to recognize that relation in reference to our second class of representations.

§ 42. Subject of Willing

From what has been said, the subject of knowing can never be known or become object or representation.

However, we have not merely an outer self-knowledge (in sensuous intuitive perception), but also an inner, and yet in consequence of its nature all knowledge presupposes a known and a knower. Thus within us the known as such is not the knower but the willer, the subject of willing, the will. Starting from knowledge we can say that "I know" is an analytical proposition, whereas "I will" is a synthetical, and moreover a posteriori, that is to say, is given by experience, here by inner experience (in other words, in time alone). To this extent the subject of willing would therefore be for us an object. When we are introspective, we always find ourselves as the *willer*. Willing, however, has many degrees from the mildest wish to passionate desire, and I have often explained, for example, in the *Two Fundamental Problems of Ethics*, "Freedom of the Will," Vol. I and elsewhere, that not only all emotions, but even all the movements of our inner nature, subsumed under the wide concept of feeling, are states of the will.

Now the identity of the subject of willing with that of knowing by virtue whereof (and indeed necessarily) the word "I" includes and indicates both, is the knot of the world (*Weltknoten*), and hence inexplicable. For to us only the relations between objects are intelligible; but of these, two can be one only insofar as they are parts of a whole. Here, on the other hand, where we are speaking of the subject, the rules for the knowing of objects no longer apply, and an actual identity of the knower with what is known as willing and hence of the subject with the object, is *immediately given*. But whoever really grasps the inexplicable nature of this identity, will with me call it the miracle "par excellence." [Tr.]³

Now just as the subjective correlative to the first class of representations is the understanding, that to the second the faculty of reason, and that to the third pure sensibility, so is the subjective correlative to this fourth class found to be the inner sense, or generally self-consciousness.

§ 43. Willing. Law of Motivation

Just because the subject of willing is immediately given in self-consciousness, it is impossible further to define or describe the nature of willing. Indeed it is the most immediate of all our knowledge; in fact this immediacy must ultimately throw light on all the other branches of knowledge which are very mediate.

With every decision that we observe in ourselves and also in others, we regard ourselves as justified in asking, why? In other words, we assume as necessary that that decision was preceded by something from which it ensued, and which we call the ground or reason, or more accurately the motive, of the resultant action. Without such a motive the action is to us just as inconceivable as is the movement of an inanimate body without a push or pull. Accordingly, the motive is one of the causes, and has already been numbered and characterized as one of them in § 20 as the third form of causality. But the whole of causality is only the form of the principle of sufficient reason in the first class of objects, and thus in the corporeal world that is given to us in external intuitive perception. There it is the bond linking changes with one another, since the cause is that which comes from without and is the condition of each event. On the other hand, the inner nature of such events remains for us a riddle, for here we are always left on the outside. We certainly see this cause necessarily produce that effect, but we do not come to know how it is really able to do this, in other words, what is going on inside. Thus we see mechanical, physical, and chemical effects, as well as those of stimuli, ensue every time on their respective causes without on that account ever thoroughly understanding the process. On the contrary, the essential element of this remains a mystery, and we then attribute it to qualities of bodies, to natural forces, and even to vital force, all of which, however, are nothing but *qualitates occultae*. Now it would be no better as regards our understanding of the movements and actions of animals and human beings, and we should see these too brought about mysteriously through their causes (motives), if we were not here afforded an insight into the inner nature of the process. Thus from our inner experience we know that this is an act of will brought about by the motive that consists in a mere representation. Thus the effect of the motive is known to us, like that of all other causes, not only from without and hence merely indirectly, but at the same time from within and quite directly, and thus in accordance with its whole mode of action. Here we stand behind the scenes, so to speak, and learn the secret of the way in which the cause produces the effect according to its innermost nature;

for here we know in quite a different way and hence by a totally different method. The result of this is the important proposition: *motivation is causality seen from within.* Accordingly, causality is presented here in quite a different way, in quite a different medium, and for quite a different kind of knowledge. It is therefore to be presented now as a special and peculiar form of our principle, which then appears as the *principle of sufficient reason of acting, principium rationis sufficientis agendi*, or more briefly, the *law of motivation.*

To look at the problem from a different angle, I here add, in reference to my philosophy generally, that, just as the law of motivation is related to that of causality as laid down in § 20, so is this fourth class of objects for the subject, and hence the will observed within ourselves, related to the first. This view is the corner-stone of my whole metaphysics.

Concerning the nature and necessity of the operation of motives, their being conditioned by the empirical individual character as well as by the individual's cognitive faculty, and other matters, I refer to my prize-essay "On the Freedom of the Will,"[4] where all these points are discussed in detail.

§ 44. Influence of the Will on Knowledge

The influence which the will exercises on knowledge is based not on causality proper, but on the identity, discussed in § 42, of the knowing with the willing subject. For the will compels knowledge to repeat representations that were once present to the intellect, generally to direct its attention to this or that object, and to evoke at pleasure any particular series of ideas. Here too the will is determined by the law of motivation according to which it is also the secret director of the so-called association of ideas. In the second volume of the *World as Will and Representation* I have devoted a special chapter (the 14th) to that association, which is itself nothing but the application of the principle of sufficient reason in its four forms to the subjective train of thought and hence to the presence of representations in our consciousness. But it is the will of the individual that sets in motion the whole mechanism, in that it urges the intellect, in accordance with the interest, i.e., the man's individual aims, to produce for its present representations those closely related thereto logically, analogically or by proximity in space or time. But here the will's activity is so direct that we often are not clearly conscious thereof. It is so rapid that at times we are not even conscious of the occasion for a representation that is thus brought about. Here it seems as though something quite unconnected with anything else has entered our consciousness. That this, however, cannot occur, is, as I have said, precisely the root of the principle of sufficient reason, and has been discussed more fully in the above-quoted chapter of my chief work. Every picture or image that is suddenly presented to our imagination, also every judgement that does not follow its previously existing ground or reason, must be produced by an act of will which has a motive, although such motive is often not perceived because it is insignificant, and the act of will is frequently not noticed because its fulfilment is so easy that this and the wish are simultaneous.

§ 45. Memory

The peculiar characteristic of the knowing subject, enabling it to obey the will the more easily in the visualization of representations, the oftener these have been present, in other words, its *capacity for being exercised*, is what we call *memory.* I cannot agree with the usual description thereof, namely a storehouse or receptacle in which we keep a stock of ready-made representations that we should thus always have, yet without always being aware of them. The voluntary and spontaneous repetition of representations that have been present becomes so easy through practice that, as soon as a link in a series of representations has come to us, we at once recall all the others, often apparently against our will. If we wish to have a simile of this characteristic quality of our faculty of representation (such as Plato gives when he compares memory to a soft mass that receives and retains impressions), the most accurate seems to be that of a piece of cloth, which after being folded frequently, again falls automatically, as it were, into the same creases. Just as through practice the body learns to obey the will, so too does the faculty of representation. A recollection or remembrance is by no means always the same representation, as the usual description assumes—one that is again produced from the storehouse, so to speak. On the contrary, a fresh representation actually arises each time, only that practice makes this particularly easy. Thus it happens that phantasms, which we think we have stored away in our memory but actually only practice through frequent repetition, are changed imperceptibly; and of this we are made aware when we again see after a long time an old familiar object, and it does not correspond exactly to the picture we have of it at that moment. This could not happen if we stored up ready-made representations. This is also why all acquired knowledge gradually fades from our memory unless we exercise or cultivate it, simply because it is the result of practice that comes from habit and knack. Thus, for instance, most scholars forget their Greek, and artists their Italian after they return home. This also explains why we recall with difficulty a name, a verse, or suchlike that was previously familar to us but was not thought of for many years; whereas when we have succeeded in recalling it, we have it once more at our disposal for several years, because the practice is now renewed. Therefore anyone acquainted with several languages should from time to time read something in each of them, whereby he retains possession thereof.

This also explains why the surroundings and events of our childhood are so deeply engraved on our memory, since as children we have only a few, and these mainly intuitive, representations and therefore constantly repeat them for the sake of occupation. With people having little ability to think for themselves, this is the case throughout their lives (indeed not only with intuitive representations but also with concepts and words). They therefore sometimes have a very good memory when such is not prevented by obtuseness and mental indolence. Men of genius, on the other hand, do not always have excellent memories, as Rousseau tells us of himself. The explanation might be that a host of new ideas and combinations leaves a man of genius no time for frequent repetitions; although it will not be easy to find a genius with a thoroughly bad memory, because the greater energy and mobility of the whole power of thought here make up for constant practice. We must also not forget that Mnemosyne is the Mother of the Muses. Accordingly, it can be said that memory is under two mutually antagonistic influences, that of the energy of the representation-faculty, on the one hand, and that of the host of representations occupying that faculty, on the other. The smaller the first factor, the smaller too must be the other in order to furnish a good memory; and the greater the second factor, the greater must be the other. This also explains why people who incessantly read novels thereby lose their memory because with them, as with men of genius, the host of representations leaves them no time or patience for repetition and practice, and here such representations are not their own ideas and combinations, but the rapidly passing ones of others; moreover they lack that which compensates the genius for want of practice. Besides the whole thing is subject to the correction that everyone has the best memory for what interests him, and the worst for everything else. And so many a great mind forgets with incredible rapidity the petty affairs and events of daily life, and likewise the people of no account with whom he has become acquainted, whereas dullards admirably retain all these details. Nevertheless, the great mind will have a good, and even marvellous, memory for the things of importance to *him*, and for that which in itself is important.

But generally speaking, it is easy to see that we best retain those series of representations that hang together on the thread of one or more of the above-mentioned species of grounds and consequents; but that it is more difficult to retain such representations as are connected not with one another, but only with our will in accordance with the law of motivation, that is, such as are arbitrarily grouped. Thus with the former representations the fact that the formal part is known to us a priori saves us half the trouble. This, like all knowledge a priori in general, probably gave rise to Plato's theory that all learning is only recollecting.

1. *Id videndum non est: omnia videt; et id audiendum non est: omnia audit; sciendum non est: omnia scit; et intelligendum non est: omnia intelligit. Praeter id, videns, et sciens, et audiens, et intelligens ens aliud non est.*

2. Ἡ ψυχὴ τὰ ὄντα πώς ἐστι πάντα *(anima quodammodo est universa, quae sunt).*

3. Κατ' ἐξοχήν.

4. The first of two ethical essays in the work *The Two Fundamental Problems of Ethics.* [Tr.]

CHAPTER VIII

GENERAL REMARKS AND RESULTS

§ 46. Systematic Arrangement

The order in which I have stated the different forms of our principle is not systematic but chosen for the sake of clearness, in order first to present that which is better known and least presupposes the rest. This is in accordance with Aristotle's rule: "Sometimes also with instruction a start must be made not from what is first and the beginning of the matter, but from what is most easily understood." [Tr.] [1] (*Metaphysics*, IV, 1.) But the following is the systematic arrangement in which the classes of grounds or reasons should follow. First, the principle of the ground or reason of being should be mentioned, and here again first its application to *time*, for time is the simple schema of all the other forms of the principle of sufficient reason, and this schema contains only what is essential; indeed time is the prototype of all finiteness. Then the ground or reason of being in space should be stated, and after this the law of causality followed by that of motivation, and finally the principle of sufficient reason or ground of knowing; for the

221

other grounds are concerned with immediate representations, whereas this last deals with representations from representations.

The truth here expressed, that time is the simple schema, containing only the essential element of all the forms of the principle of sufficient reason, explains the absolutely perfect clearness and precision of arithmetic, a point in which no other science can compete with it. Thus all sciences are based on the principle of sufficient reason, since they are without exception combinations of grounds and consequents. Now the series of numbers is the simple and only one of the grounds and consequents of being in time; on account of this perfect simplicity, for besides it there is nothing, nor are there anywhere any indefinite relations, it leaves nothing to be desired as regards accuracy, apodictic certainty, and clearness. In this respect arithmetic surpasses all the other sciences, even geometry, because so many relations arise from the three dimensions of space that their survey becomes too difficult for empirical intuitive perception as well as for pure intuition. Therefore complex problems in geometry are solved only by calculation, and thus geometry is quick to resolve itself into arithmetic. It is not necessary for me to show that the other sciences contain many different elements of obscurity.

§ 47. Time Relation Between Ground and Consequent

According to the laws of causality and motivation, the

ground must precede the consequent as regards time. This is absolutely essential, as I have fully explained in the second volume of my chief work, Chapter 4; and to this I refer in order to avoid repetition. Accordingly, as soon as we bear in mind that it is not one thing which is the cause of another thing, but one state which is the cause of another state, we shall not let ourselves be misled by examples such as the one mentioned by Kant (*Critique of Pure Reason*, 1st ed., p. 202; 5th ed., p. 248), that the stove, which is the cause of the heat in a room, is simultaneous with its effect (the heat). The state of the stove, that it has a temperature higher than that of its surrounding medium, must precede the communication thereto of its surplus heat. Now as each layer of air on becoming warm makes way for a cooler layer streaming in, the first state, the cause, and consequently also the second, the effect, are renewed so long as the stove and the room do not have the same temperature. Here, then, we do not have a permanent cause (the stove), and a permanent effect (the heat of the room) that are simultaneous, but a chain of changes, a constant renewing of two states, one of which is the effect of the other. From this example we can, of course, see how confused was even Kant's conception of causality.

On the other hand, the principle of sufficient reason of knowing does not entail a relation in time, but only one for our faculty of reason; therefore *before* and *after* are here without any meaning.

In the same way there is no relation of time in the principle of sufficient reason of being, insofar as this principle is valid in geometry, but only a spatial relation of which it might be said that everything would be simultaneous, if simultaneity as well as succession were here not without any meaning. In arithmetic, on the other hand, the ground of being is nothing but just the time relation itself.

§ 48. Reciprocity of Grounds and Reasons

The principle of sufficient reason in each of its meanings can establish a hypothetical judgement, just as indeed every such judgement ultimately depends on this principle; and here the laws of hypothetical conclusions always remain valid. Thus it is correct to infer the existence of the consequent from the existence of the ground, and the nonexistence of the ground from the nonexistence of the consequent. But it is wrong to infer the nonexistence of the consequent from the nonexistence of the ground, and the existence of the ground from the existence of the consequent. Now it is remarkable that in geometry we are nevertheless almost always able to infer the existence of the ground from the existence of the consequent, and the nonexistence of the consequent from the nonexistence of the ground. This is because, as was shown in § 37, every line determines the position of the others, and here it is immaterial from which we begin, that is to say, which we consider as ground and which as consequent. Of this we can convince ourselves by going through all the geometrical theorems. It is only when we are considering not merely figures, i.e., the positions of lines, but areas apart from figures, that we are unable in most cases to infer the existence of the ground from the existence of the consequent, or rather to reciprocate the propositions and make the conditioned the condition. An example of this is the proposition: Triangles having equal bases and equal heights are equal in area. This cannot be converted into: Triangles equal in area have also equal bases and equal heights; for the heights can be in inverse proportion to the bases.

It was mentioned in § 20 that the law of causality does not admit of reciprocity, since the effect can never be the cause of its cause, and so according to its proper meaning the concept of reciprocity is inadmissible. Under the principle of sufficient reason of knowing, a reciprocity would be possible only with convertible or reciprocal concepts, since only their spheres cover each other; moreover it gives a *circulus vitiosus.*[2]

§ 49. Necessity

The principle of sufficient reason in all its form is the sole principle and sole support of all necessity. For *necessity* has no true and clear meaning except that of the inevitability of the consequent with the positing of the ground. Accordingly, every necessity is *conditioned;* absolute or unconditioned necessity is therefore a *contradictio in adjecto.*[3] For *to be necessary* can never mean anything but to follow from a given ground or reason. If, on the other hand, we try to define it as "what is unable not to be," we give a mere verbal explanation, and take refuge behind an extremely abstract concept in order to avoid a real definition of the thing. But we can be driven at once from this position by the question how it is then possible or even conceivable for anything to be incapable of not being, for indeed all existence is given merely empirically. The result then is that it is possible only insofar as there is posited or present some *ground* or *reason* from which it follows. Consequently, to be necessary and to follow from a given ground or reason are convertible terms, and as such can always be substituted, the one by the other. Thus the concept of the "*ABSOLUTELY necessary being*," which is such a favourite with pseudo-philosophers, contains a contradiction. Through the predicate "*absolute*" (in other words, "dependent on nothing else"), it eliminates the only determination whereby "*necessary*" is conceivable and has any meaning. Here again we have an example of the *improper use of abstract concepts* for the purpose of metaphysical manoeuvering. I have pointed out similar instances of this in the concepts "*immaterial substance*," "*absolute ground or reason*," "*cause in general*," and so on.* I cannot too often repeat that all abstract concepts must be controlled by *intuitive perception*.

Accordingly, there is a fourfold necessity corresponding to the four forms of the principle of sufficient reason. (1) *Logical necessity*, according to the principle of sufficient reason of knowing, by virtue whereof, when once we have admitted the premisses, the conclusion must be admitted without question. (2) Physical necessity, according to the law of causality, by virtue whereof, as soon as the cause has appeared, the effect cannot fail to appear. (3) Mathematical necessity, according to the principle of sufficient reason of being, by virtue whereof every relation, stated by a true geometrical theorem, is as that theorem affirms it to be, and every correct calculation remains irrefutable. (4) Moral necessity, by virtue whereof every human being, even every animal, after the motive has appeared, must carry out the action which alone is in accordance with his inborn and immutable character. This action then ensues just as inevitably as does every other effect of a cause, although on account of the difficulty of fathoming and completely knowing the individual empirical character and its allotted sphere of knowledge, it is not so easy to predict, as with every other cause, what the action will be. To investigate this is different from getting to know the properties of a neutral salt, and thus predicting its reaction. I cannot too often repeat this because of the dunces and duffers who, for the benefit of their petticoat philosophy, still persist in boldly asserting the contrary, in spite of the unanimous teaching of so many great minds. Of course, I am no professor of philosophy who is obliged to bow and scrape to the folly and stupidity of others.

§ 50. Series of Grounds and Consequents

According to the law of causality, the condition is

again always conditioned, moreover in the same way; hence there arises a *series in infinitum a parte ante.*[4] It is the same with the ground of being in space; every relative space is a figure; it has limits whereby it is connected with another relative space, and which again condition the figure of this other, and so ad infinitum in all dimensions. But if we consider a single figure in itself, the series of grounds of being has an end, because we have started from a given relation; just as the series of causes comes to an end when we stop at any arbitrarily chosen cause. In time the series of grounds of being has infinite extension both *a parte ante* and *a parte post,*[4] since each moment is conditioned by a previous one, and necessarily brings about the following; hence time cannot have either beginning or end. The series of grounds of knowledge, on the other hand, that is to say, a series of judgements, each of which gives logical truth to the other, always ends somewhere, thus in an empirical, transcendental, or metalogical truth. If the ground of the major proposition, to which we have been led, is the first judgement and hence an empirical truth, and we continue to ask why, then what we now demand is no longer a ground of knowledge, but a cause; in other words, the series of the grounds of knowing passes over into that of the grounds of becoming. But when once we do the reverse and allow the series of the grounds of becoming to pass over into that of the grounds of knowing so that it can come to an end, then this is never brought about by the nature of the thing, but by a special intention and so by a trick. Indeed it is the well-known sophism called the ontological proof. Thus after we have arrived through the cosmological proof at a cause at which we would like to stop in order to make it the first, the law of causality for all that cannot be brought to a standstill, but will go on asking why. It is therefore secretly set aside, and the principle of sufficient reason of knowing, which at a distance resembles the law of causality, is put in its place. Thus instead of the cause here demanded, a ground of knowledge is given which is drawn from the concept itself—a concept to be demonstrated and therefore still problematical as to its reality. And this ground of knowledge, since indeed it is a ground or reason, must now figure as a cause. That concept has naturally been previously arranged for this purpose, since reality, wrapped up in a few garments possibly for the sake of decency, was laid in it, and so the delightful surprise of now finding it there was prepared. All this was previously discussed in § 7. On the other hand, if a chain of judgements rests ultimately on a proposition of transcendental or metalogical truth and we still go on asking why, then to this there is no answer, because the question has no meaning and thus does not know what kind of a ground it demands. For the principle of sufficient reason or ground is the *principle of all explanation*. To explain a thing means to reduce its given existence or connexion to some form of the principle of sufficient reason. According to this form, that existence or connexion must be as it is. The result of this is that the principle of sufficient reason itself, in other words, the connexion expressed by it in any of its forms, cannot be further explained, since there is no principle for explaining the principle of all explanation; just as the eye sees everything except itself. It is true that there are series of

229

motives, since the resolve to attain an end becomes the
motive for the resolve to use a whole series of means. Yet
this series always ends *a parte priori* in a representation
from the first two classes, where we find the motive that
was originally able to set this individual will in motion.
Now the fact that the motive could do this, is a datum for
knowing the empirical character here given; but we cannot
say why this character is moved by that motive, because the
intelligible character lies outside time and never becomes an
object. Therefore the series of motives as such comes to an
end in such a final motive, and, according as its last link was
a real object or a mere concept, it passes over into the series
of causes or the series of grounds of knowledge.

§ 51. Every Science Has for its Guidance One of the Forms of the Principle of Sufficient Reason Rather than the Others

The question why always wants a sufficient ground or
reason, and the connexion of the different parts of
knowledge according to the principle of sufficient reason
distinguishes science from the mere aggregate of such parts;
it was therefore stated in § 4 that the Why is the mother of the
sciences. It is also found that in each branch of science one
of the forms of our principle rather than the others is the
guiding line, although in that branch the other forms also
apply, yet in a more subordinate role. Thus in pure

mathematics the ground of being is the chief guide (although in the proofs the demonstration proceeds only on the ground of knowledge); in applied mathematics the law of causality appears at the same time; and this law gains complete supremacy in physics, chemistry, geology and other sciences. The principle of sufficient reason of knowing finds intensive application throughout all the branches of science, for in all the particular is known from the general. But it is the chief guide and almost supreme in botany, zoology, mineralogy, and other classifying sciences. The law of motivation is the main guide for history, politics, pragmatic psychology, and so on, if we consider all motives and maxims, whatever they be, as data for explaining actions; if, however, we make the motives and maxims themselves as regards their value and origin the subject of our investigation, the law of motivation becomes the guide for ethics. In the second volume of my chief work, Chapter 12, is found the main classification of the sciences in accordance with this principle.

§ 52. Two Main Results

In this essay I have attempted to show that the principle of sufficient reason or ground is a common expression for four entirely different relations each of which rests on a particular law that is given a priori (for the principle of sufficient reason is synthetical a priori). Ac-

231

echo of p. 1

cording to the principle of *homogeneity*, it must be assumed of these four laws that are found according to the principle of *specification*, that, as they combine in one common expression, they also spring from one and the same original quality of our whole cognitive faculty as their common root. Accordingly, this root would have to be regarded as the innermost germ of all the dependence, relativity, instability, and finiteness of the objects of our consciousness or the world. Such a consciousness is confined to sensibility, understanding, faculty of reason, subject and object, and such a world is repeatedly degraded by the sublime Plato to the "always only arising and passing away, but never really and truly existing," [Tr.][5] the knowledge of which would be only "a mere thinking or supposing by means of irrational or senseless perception." [Tr.][6] With a correct instinct Christianity calls the world *temporal* in accordance with that form of our principle which I have described in § 46 as its simplest schema and the prototype of all finiteness. The general meaning of the principle of sufficient reason may, on the whole, be reduced to the fact that always and everywhere each thing exists merely *by virtue of another thing*. But the principle of sufficient reason is a priori in all its forms, and thus has its roots in our intellect. Therefore, it cannot be applied to the totality of all existing things, to the world, including the intellect in which the world presents itself. For such a world that presents itself by virtue of a priori forms is precisely on that account a mere phenomenon. Therefore what holds good of world merely in consequence of those very forms, cannot be applied to the world itself, in other words, to the thing-in-itself that manifests itself in the world. And so we cannot say that "the world and all things therein exist by virtue of something else"; such a proposition is simply the cosmological proof.

If in the present essay I have succeeded in deducing the result just expressed, it would seem to me that every philosopher, who in his speculations bases a conclusion on the principle of sufficient reason or ground, or indeed speaks of a ground at all, should be required to state what kind of ground he means. One would imagine that, whenever there was any talk of a ground or reason, this would be done as a matter of course, and that no confusion would be possible. But only too often we find examples in some of which the expressions ground, reason, and cause are confused and used indiscriminately, whereas in others there is talk in a *general* way of a basis and of something based, of *principia* and *principiata*, of condition and of what is conditioned, without further specification, possibly because there is a secret awareness of an unauthorized use of these concepts. Thus even Kant speaks of the thing-in-itself as the *ground* or *reason* of the phenomenon. In the *Critique of Pure Reason*, 5th ed., p. 590, he speaks of a *ground* or *reason* of the *possibility* of all phenomena, of an *intelligible ground* of the phenomena, of an *intelligible cause*, of an *unknown ground* of the possibility of the sensuous series in general (p. 592), of a *transcendental object as the ground* of phenomena, and of the *ground or reason* why our sensibility should have this rather than all the other principal conditions (p. 641), and this in several places. All this does not seem to me to be in keeping with those weighty, profound, indeed immortal words (p. 591): "that the contingency[7] of things is *itself only phenomenon*, and can lead to no other than the empirical regressus that determines phenomena."

Anyone acquainted with the more recent works on philosophy knows that, since Kant, the concepts ground and consequent, *principia* and *principiata*, and so on are used much more indefinitely and in a wholly transcendent sense.

The following is my objection to this confused and indefinite use of the words *ground* or *reason*, and also of the principle of sufficient reason generally. At the same time it is the second result which is closely connected with the first and is given by this essay on its subject matter. The four laws of our cognitive faculty, whose common expression is the principle of sufficient reason or ground, are declared through their common character and by the fact that all objects of the subject are allotted to them, as established by one and the same primary quality and inner peculiarity of our cognitive faculty, a faculty that appears as sensibility, understanding, and power of reason (*Vernunft*). Therefore, even if we imagined that a new fifth class of objects could come about, we should likewise have to assume that in this class the principle of sufficient reason would also appear in a new form. Nevertheless we still have no right to speak of an *absolute ground or reason*, and there is no more a *ground in general* than there is a *triangle in general* except in an abstract concept that is obtained through discursive thinking. As a representation from representations, such a concept is nothing but a means for thinking many things through one. Just as every triangle must be acute-angled, right-angled, or obtuse-angled, equilateral, isosceles, or scalene, so must every ground or reason belong to one of the four possible kinds previously mentioned (for we have only four definitely separate classes of objects). Accordingly, every ground or reason must be valid within one of those four possible classes of objects of our representation faculty; consequently, the use of this ground or reason assumes as given one of those possible classes together with that faculty, that is, with the whole world, and it keeps within these limits. But such a ground or reason cannot be valid outside its possible class, or even outside of all objects. If, however, anyone should think differently about this and imagine that ground or reason in general is something different from the concept which is drawn from the four kinds of grounds and expresses what is common to them, we might renew the controversy of the Realists and Nominalists, and in the present case I should have to side with the latter.

Footnotes

1. Καὶ μαθήσεως οὐκ ἀπὸ τοῦ πρώτου, καὶ τῆς τοῦ πράγματος ἀρχῆς ἐνίοτε ἀρκτέον, ἀλλ' ὅθεν ῥᾷστ' ἂν μάθοι. (*Et doctrina non a primo, ac rei principio aliquando inchoanda est, sed unde quis facilius discat.*)

2. "Vicious circle." [Tr.]

3. "A logical inconsistency between a noun and its modifying adjective" [such as "a round square," "wooden iron," "cold fire," "hot snow." Tr.]

*On "immaterial substance" compare *World as Will and Representation*, Vol. I, "Criticism of the Kantian Philosophy"; and on "absolute ground or reason" § 52 of the present work. [Note added by Julius Frauenstädt. Tr.]

4. *A parte ante*, from the side of the before, referring to duration previous to a given event or point. *A parte post*, from the side of the after, referring to duration subsequent to a given event or point. [Tr.]

5. Ἀεὶ γιγνόμενον μὲν καὶ ἀπολλύμενον, ὄντως δὲ οὐδέποτε ὄν.

6. Δόξα μετ' αἰσθήσεως ἀλόγου.

7. Empirical contingency is meant which with Kant signifies as much as dependence on other things. On this point I refer to the censure in my "Criticism of the Kantian Philosophy."

APPENDIX[1]

ON VISION

Intellectual Nature of Intuitive Perception. Distinction Between Understanding and Faculty of Reason, Between Illusion and Error. Knowledge the Characteristic of Animal Life. Application of All that is Stated to Intuitive Perception Through the Eye

All intuitive perception is intellectual, for without the *understanding* we could never achieve perception, the apprehension of *objects*. On the contrary, we should stop short at the mere sensation which might possibly have meaning in reference to the will as pain or comfort; but for the rest it would be a succession of state devoid of meaning, and nothing like knowledge. Intuitive perception, i.e., knowledge of an *object*, first comes about through the *understanding* which refers every impression received by the body to its *cause*. In space that is intuitively perceived a priori the understanding shifts this cause to the point from where the effects starts and thus recognizes the cause as acting, as *actual*, i.e., as a representation of the same kind and class as the body. But this transition from the effect to the cause is direct, vivid, and necessary, for it is a knowledge of the *pure understanding*. It is not a rational conclusion, a combination of concepts and judgements according to logical laws. Such a combination is rather the business of the *faculty of reason* which contributes nothing to intuitive perception, but whose object is quite a different class of representations. In this world such a class belongs solely to the human race; they are abstract, not intuitive, representations; in other words, they are *concepts*. But through these man is given his great advantages such as speech, science, and above all that reflectiveness which is possible only by surveying the whole of life in concepts, and which keeps him independent of the impression of the present moment, and thus enables him to act with premeditation, deliberation, and method. In this way his actions differ so vastly from those of the animals, and finally there is also that condition for deliberate choice between several motives by virtue whereof the decisions of his will are accompanied by the most complete self-consciousness. For all this man is indebted to *concepts*, i.e., to the *faculty of reason.* As an abstract principle the law of causality is naturally, like all principles *in abstracto*, reflection, and hence an object of the faculty of reason. But the real, vivid, direct, and necessary knowledge of the law of causality precedes all reflection, as it does all experience, and is to be found in the *understanding*. By means of such knowledge the body's sensations become the starting-point for the intuitive perception of a world, in that the law of causality (known to us a priori) is applied to the relation between the immediate object (the body) and all other objects that are merely mediate. Knowledge of the same law applied solely to and among mediate objects gives us cleverness when it attains a higher degree of keenness and precision; and this can be just as little produced by abstract

238

concepts as can intuitive perception generally. Therefore to be rational and to be clever are two very different qualities.

Thus intuitive perception, knowledge of objects, of an objective world, is the work of the understanding. The senses are merely the seat of an enhanced sensibility; they are parts of the body which in a higher degree are susceptible to the influence of other bodies. Moreover, each sense is open to a particular kind of influence to which the other senses are either slightly susceptible or not so at all. This specific difference of sensation of each of the five senses has its ground not in the nervous system itself, but only in the way in which this system is affected. We can therefore regard each sensation as a modification of the sense of touch or of the ability to feel which extends over the whole body. For the substance of the nerves (apart from the sympathetic system) is in the whole body one and the same without the slightest difference. Now when it is affected by light through the eye or sound through the ear, and receives such specifically different sensations, this cannot reside within the substance itself, but only in the way in which it is affected. But this depends partly on the outside agent by which it is affected (light, sound, odour), and partly on the mechanism by which it is exposed to the impression of this agent, i.e., on the organ of sense. The fact that in the ear the nerve of the labyrinth and cochlea, floating in the auditory fluid, receives the vibrations of air by means of this fluid, but that the optic nerve receives the effect of light through the aqueous humour and the crystalline lens breaking up the light in the eye, is the cause of the specific difference of the two sensations, not the nerve itself.[2] Accordingly, even the auditory nerve could see and the optic nerve hear, if the external apparatus of both were to change places. However, the modification undergone by the senses through such influence is not yet by any means an intuitive perception, but only the material which the understanding converts into such a perception. Of all the senses, that of sight is capable of the most delicate and diverse impressions from without; yet in itself it can give only sensation which first becomes intuitive perception through the application of the understanding to it. If anyone standing before a beautiful landscape could for a moment be deprived of all understanding, then for him nothing of the whole view would be left but the sensation of a very manifold affection of his retina, resembling the many blobs of different colours on an artist's palette. These are, so to speak, the raw material from which just a moment previously his understanding created that intuitive perception.[3] In the first weeks of life the child feels with all his senses; he does not intuitively perceive, does not apprehend; he therefore stares stupidly at the world. Yet he soon begins to learn the use of his understanding, to apply the law of causality that is known to him prior to all experience, and to combine this with the forms of all knowledge, time and space, which are likewise given a priori. Thus from sensation he arrives at intuitive perception, at apprehension, and he then looks at the world with shrewd, discerning, and intelligent eyes. But each object operates differently on all five senses, and yet these effects lead back to one and the same cause which precisely in this way presents itself as object. Therefore the child learning intuitive perception compares the different kinds of impressions which he receives from the same object. He touches what he sees and examines what he touches; according to the sound he proceeds to the cause thereof. He brings to his aid smell and taste; finally for his eye he also takes into account distance and illumination. He becomes acquainted with the effect of light and shade, and in the end, after much effort, also becomes familiar with perspective, knowledge of which is brought about through the union of the laws of space with the law of causality. These two reside a priori in consciousness and require only application. Now here we must take into account even the changes undergone partly by the inner conformation of the eyes and partly by the mutual position of the two eyes when they see at different distances. All these combinations are already made for the understanding by ,the child, but for the faculty of reason, i.e., *in abstracto* only by the optician. Thus the child elaborates the manifold data of sensibility into *intuitive perception* in accordance with the laws of the *understanding* that are known to him a priori. With that perception the world first of all exists for him as an object. Much later he learns to use the *faculty of reason*; he then begins to understand speech, to talk, and to *think* in the real sense of the word.

What is here said about intuitive perception will be even more illuminating from a more detailed consideration of the matter. The very first requirement for the acquisition of intuitive perception is that objects stand upright, whereas their impression is upside down. Thus since the rays of light coming from a body cross when they pass through the pupil, the impression which they make on the nervous substance of the retina, and which has been erroneously called its image, comes through in an inverted order. Thus light coming from the bottom arrives at the top, that from the top at the bottom, that from the right arrives on the left, and vice versa. Now if, as was assumed, an actual image on the retina were the object of intuitive perception which was then brought about in some way by a soul sitting at the back of the brain, then we should see the object inverted, as actually happens in every camera which receives through a mere hole the light from external objects. Here it is not so; but intuitive perception is brought about by the fact that the understanding instantly refers the impression felt on the retina to its cause which then precisely in this way presents itself as an object in space that is its accompanying form of intuition. By thus going back from the effect to the cause, the understanding follows the direction that is inevitably followed by the sensation of the rays of light. Thus everything is back again in its right place, for what was in the sensation at the bottom now appears in the object at the top. The second essential for the acquisition of intuitive perception is that, although the child sees with two eyes, each of which receives a so-called image of the object, and indeed in such a way that the direction from the same point of the object to each eye is different, he nevertheless learns to see only *one* object. This occurs simply by virtue of the original knowledge of the law of causality, whereby the effect of a point of light is recognized as causally originating from *one* point and object, although it impinges on each eye in a different direction. The two lines from that point through the pupils onto each retina are called the optical axes, and their angle at that point is the optical angle. If, when observing an object, each eye-ball in respect of its orbit has the same position as the other, as is the case in the normal state, then in each of the two eyes the optical axis will rest on *mutually corresponding, homonymous* spots of the retina. Here it is not the outer side of one retina that corresponds to that of the other, but the right side of the left retina that corresponds to the right side of the right, and so on. With this regular position of the eyes in their orbits, which is always maintained in all the natural movements of the eyes, we now become empirically acquainted with the spots which exactly correspond to one another on the two retinas, and henceforth refer the affections originating on these analogous spots always to one and the same object as their cause. Therefore, although we see with two eyes and receive double impressions, we cognize and perceive everything only singly. That which is *doubly felt through the senses* is only *singly perceived intuitively*, just because intuitive perception is intellectual and not merely sensuous. But it is the conformity of the affected spots of each retina to which we agree in the case of that *conclusion of the understanding*. This can be proved from the fact that, while the optical axes arc directed to a more distant object and this closes the optical angle, an object standing nearer to us appears double, just because the light coming therefrom through the pupils onto the retinas now impinges on two spots that are not analogous. Conversely, for the same reason, the more distant object is seen double if we direct our eyes to the nearer object and close the optical angle thereto. In the second edition of my essay *On the Fourfold Root* there is a plate that gives a graphic description of the matter and is very useful for a thorough comprehension thereof. In Robert Smith's *Optics*, Cambridge, 1738, will be found a detailed description, illustrated with many figures, of the different positions of the optical axes and of the phenomena thereby produced.

This relation between the optical axes and the object is at bottom no different from the case where the impression which is made on each of the ten fingers by a body that is touched, and which differs in accordance with the position of each finger in contact with it, is nevertheless perceived and recognized as resulting from *one* body. Knowledge of an object never results from the mere impression, but always only from the application thereto of the law of causality, and consequently of the understanding. Incidentally, it is thus very absurd to represent knowledge of the law of causality as springing first from experience, for example, from the resistance offered by bodies to our pressure. For the law of causality is the sole form of the understanding and the condition of the possibility of any objective perception. It is also the preliminary condition of our perception of those bodies; and this again must first be the motive of our acting on them. And if the understanding did not already possess the law of causality and bring it ready-made to the sensation, how then could that motive arise from the mere feeling of a pressure in the hands which does not resemble it at all? (On causality between the will and bodily action, see *World as Will and Representation*,

Vol. II, Chap. 4, and *On the Fourfold Root of the Principle of Sufficient Reason*.)[4] If Englishmen and Frenchmen are still burdened with such buffoonery, we can put this down to their artless innocence, since the Kantian philosophy has not yet sunk into them and they are therefore still involved in the inadequate empiricism of Locke and Condillac. But today German philosophasters presume to pass off time, space, and causality as knowledge of experience, and again offer for sale suchlike absurdities which for seventy years have been completely set aside and exploded, and at which even their grandfathers shrugged their shoulders (in the meantime there lurk behind such marketing certain designs which I have exposed in the preface to the second edition of *On the Will in Nature*). They therefore deserve to be confronted with the *Xenien* of Goethe and Schiller:

> "Poor empirical devil! you do not even know
> The dulness in you; it is alas so *a priori* dull."

In particular I advise everyone unfortunate enough to possess a copy of the third edition of Ernst Reinhold's *System der Metaphysik*, 1854 to write this verse on the title-page. Just because the a priori nature of the law of causality is so obvious, even Goethe speaks of "the *most inborn conception*, the most necessary of cause and effect"; and he was not otherwise concerned with investigations of this sort, and merely followed his own feelings. (Cf. *Ueber Naturwissenschaft im Allgemeinen* in the tenth volume of his posthumous works.) However, I return to our theory of empirical intuitive perception.

After intuitive perception has long been acquired, there

can occur a very remarkable case which furnishes, as it were, a proof of all that has been said. Thus after we have practised at every moment for many years the business (learnt in childhood) of elaborating and arranging the data of sensibility in accordance with the laws of the understanding, such data can become confused through a change in the position of our organs of sense. Two cases in which this occurs are well known, namely shifting the eyes from their regular natural position as in squinting, and crossing the middle and index fingers of one hand. We now see and touch *one* object as *double*. As always, the understanding correctly goes to work, but it receives nothing but false data. For the rays of light proceeding from the same point to the two eyes no longer impinge on the two retinas at mutually corresponding spots; and the outer sides of the two fingers touch the opposite surfaces of the same ball, which could never happen with the natural position of the fingers. The results of this are double sight and double touch as a false illusion which cannot possibly be removed, since the understanding does not at once abandon again the application so laboriously acquired, but still always assumes the position of the sense organs which hitherto prevailed. But an even more striking proof of our theory, because it is more unusual, is furnished by the opposite case in which we see *two* objects as *one*. This occurs when each of the objects is seen with a different eye, but affects in each eye the homonymous spots of the retina—spots that correspond to those in the other eye. Arrange two similar cardboard tubes parallel to each other so that the distance between them is equal to that between the eyes. Fix a coin vertically in the object end of each tube. If we now look through the tubes with both eyes, we shall see only *one* tube and *one* coin, because the optical axes cannot close the optical angle that would be suitable to this distance. On the contrary, the axes remain quite parallel, since each follows its tube, whereby in each eye the corresponding spots of the retina are now affected by a different coin. The understanding then attributes this double impression to one and the same object, and therefore apprehends only one object where there are nevertheless two. The recently invented stereoscope also depends on this. For this purpose two photographs are taken of the same object, yet with a slight difference in the position thereof, which corresponds to the parallax from one eye to the other. They are now placed side by side at the very obtuse angle suitable to this parallax, and are then looked at through the binocular tube. The results are (1) that the symmetrically corresponding spots of the two retinas are affected by the same points of the two pictures; and (2) that each of the two eyes sees on the picture in front of it *that* part of the photographed body which, on account of the parallax of its view-point, remains covered from the other eye. In this way we get not only the two pictures merging into one in the intuitive apprehension of the understanding, but also, in consequence of the second circumstance, the perfect manifestation of a solid body. A mere painting, even one produced by the greatest art and skill, never produces such an illusion, because it always shows us its objects only as a one-eyed person would see them. I do not know how a proof of the intellectual nature of intuitive perception could be more striking.

Without a knowledge of this, we shall never understand the stereoscope, but shall make futile and fruitless attempts with purely physiological explanations.

We now see that all these illusions result from the fact that the data, to which the understanding learnt in earliest infancy to apply its laws and has throughout its life become accustomed, are shifted for it, in that they are placed in a position different from that which they occupy in the natural course of things. But at the same time, this consideration offers so clear a view of the difference between the faculties of understanding and reason, that I cannot refrain from drawing attention thereto. Thus it is true that for the faculty of reason such an illusion can be removed, but it cannot be destroyed for the understanding which, just because it is pure understanding, is irrational. What I mean is that with such an illusion intentionally arranged we *know* quite well *in abstracto*, and thus for the *faculty of reason*, that, for example, only *one* object exists, although we see and touch two respectively with crossed eyes and fingers; or that two exist, although we see only *one*. But in spite of this abstract knowledge the illusion itself still persists fixed and unmoved. For understanding and sensibility are inaccessible to the principles of the faculty of reason, in other words, they are just void of reason. From this we see what *illusion* and *error* really are; the former is deception of the *understanding*, the latter that of the *faculty of reason*; the former is opposed to *reality*, the latter to *truth*. Illusion invariably results from the fact that to the always regular and unalterable apprehension of the *understanding* is attributed a state of the organs of sense which is unusual, in other words, is different from the one to which it has learnt to apply its functions. Or again illusion arises from the fact that an effect which the senses receive normally every day and hour from one and the same cause, is for once produced by an entirely different cause. This happens, for instance, when we mistake a painting for a relievo; or a stick plunged into water appears broken; or a concave mirror shows an object as floating in front of it, a convex one showing it as behind; or the moon appears much larger on the horizon than at its zenith. This is due not to refraction, but simply to the direct assessment of its size which is carried out by the understanding according to distance, and this again, as with terrestrial objects, according to atmospheric perspective, i.e., to cloudiness through vapour and smoke. *Error* on the other hand, is a *judgement of the faculty of reason* (*Vernunft*) which does *not* stand to something outside it in that relation required by the principle of sufficient reason or ground (*Grund*) in that form in which it holds good for the faculty of reason as such; thus error is an actual, yet false judgement, a groundless assumption *in abstracto*. Illusion can give rise to error, as for instance in the case already quoted the judgement: "here are two balls" which stands to nothing in the aforesaid relation, and thus has no ground. On the other hand, the judgement: "I feel an effect similar to that of two balls" is true, for it stands to the felt affection in the above-mentioned relation. Error can be effaced precisely through a judgement which is true and has the illusion as its ground, in other words, through a statement of the illusion as such. Illusion, however, cannot be eliminated; for instance, the moon does not become smaller because of the abstract knowledge of the faculty of reason (*Vernunft*) that an estimation according to atmospheric perspective and the greater density of smoke and vapour in a horizontal direction make it larger. Nevertheless the illusion may gradually disappear when its cause is permanent, and the unusual thereby becomes the usual. If, for example, a man has his eyes in the position of a squint, his understanding tries to correct its apprehension and to produce through a correct grasp of the external cause an agreement between perceptions obtained in different ways, thus between seeing and touching. It then does afresh what it did in the child, and now becomes acquainted with the spots on each retina which, with the new position of the eyes, are now affected by the ray of light coming from *one* point. Therefore the man with a permanent squint still sees everything singly. But if through an accident, such as paralysis of the eye muscles, a man is *suddenly* forced into a constant squint, then to begin with he continues to see everything double. As evidence of this, there is the case reported by Cheselden (*Anatomy*, 3d ed., p. 324) where a man received a blow on the head, and his eyes assumed a permanently distorted position. He now saw everything double, but after some time he again had single vision, although his eyes remained out of parallel. A similar case is found in the *Ophthalmologische Bibliothek*, Vol. III, Pt. 3, p. 164. If the patient described therein had not made a quick recovery, he would have had a permanent squint, but in the end would no longer have seen double. Yet another case of this kind is related by Home in his lecture in the *Philosophical*

Transactions for 1797. Likewise a man who always kept his fingers crossed would in the end cease to have a double touch. But so long as a man squints each day at a different optical angle, he will see everything double. For the rest, it may always be as Buffon states (*Histoire de l'académie des sciences*, 1743) that those with a very pronounced and inward squint do not see at all with the distorted eye; but this will not apply to all cases of squinting.

Now as there is no intuitive perception without understanding, all animals undoubtedly have this mental faculty. In fact understanding distinguishes animals from plants, just as the faculty of reason does human beings from animals. For *knowledge* is the really outstanding *characteristic of animal life*, and this positively calls for understanding. Many different attempts have been made to establish a sign of distinction between animals and plants, but nothing entirely satisfactory has ever been found. The most felicitous expression was always *motus spontaneus in victu sumendo.*[5] But this is only a phenomenon established by knowledge and thus subordinate thereto. For a truly arbitrary and spontaneous movement, not resulting from mechanical, chemical, or physiological causes, takes place entirely in accordance with a *known object* which becomes the *motive* of that movement. Even when the polyp, that animal standing nearest to the plant, seizes its prey with its tentacles and directs it to its mouth, it has seen and perceived it (although as yet without separate eyes); and without understanding it would never have reached even this intuitive perception. The intuitively perceived object is the motive of the polyp's movement. I would therefore lay down the following distinction between inorganic body, plant, and animal. *Inorganic body* is that thing whose every movement, takes place from an external cause. In accordance with its degree, the cause is equal to the effect, so that from the cause the effect can be measured and calculated. The effect also produces in the cause an absolutely equal counter-effect. *Plant* is that which has movements whose causes, according to their degree, are by no means equal to the effects. These causes afford no measure or standard for the effects, nor do they undergo an equal counter-effect; such causes are called *stimuli*. Not only the movements of sensitive plants and of the *hedysarum gyrans*, but all assimilation, growth, tendency to light and so in plants are movement on stimuli. Finally, *animal* is that which has movements ensuing not directly and simply in accordance with the law of causality, but in accordance with that of motivation; and motivation is causality that has passed through knowledge and has this as its intermediary. Consequently, an animal is simply that which knows, and *knowledge is the real and proper characteristic of animal life*. It must not be urged that knowledge cannot furnish us with any characteristic feature because, finding ourselves outside the being to be judged, we cannot say whether or not it knows. This we certainly can do, for we can judge whether the thing on which its movements ensue acted on it as *stimulus* or *motive*; of this we can never be left in any doubt. For although stimuli differ from causes in the way I have mentioned, they nevertheless have in common with them the fact that, in order to operate, they always need contact, often even intussusception, but invariably a certain duration and intensity of impression. On the other hand, the object operating as a motive needs only to be perceived, it matters not for how long, at what distance, or how distinctly, the moment it is actually perceived. It goes without saying that in many respects the animal is at the same time plant and even inorganic body. This very important distinction of the three stages of causality, which is presented here only briefly and aphoristically, is found discussed specifically and in more detail in *The Two Fundamental Problems of Ethics*, "Freedom of the Will," Chap. 3, and also in the second edition of the essay *On the Fourfold Root of the Principle of Sufficient Reason*, § 20.

Finally, I now come to that which contains a reference of what has been so far said to our theme proper, namely *colours*, and thus proceed to a very special and subordinate part of the intuitive perception of the corporeal world. For just as the intellectual share of intuitive perception, hitherto considered, is really the function of the brain, namely of a considerable mass of nerves weighing from three to five pounds, so in the following chapter I have to consider simply the function of the fine nervous membrane at the back of the eye-ball, namely the *retina*. I shall show that the retina's specially modified activity is colour which perhaps as something additional and superfluous clothes intuitively perceived bodies. Thus the intuitive perception, i.e., apprehension, of an objective corporeal world filling space with its three dimensions, originates, as was previously pointed out in general but discussed in more detail in § 21 of the aforesaid essay *On the Fourfold Root*, through the understanding, for the understanding, and in the understanding. Like space and time, the forms underlying the understanding, it is a function of the brain. The senses are merely the points of departure for this intuitive perception of the world. Their modifications are therefore given prior to all intuitive perception; as mere sensations they are the data from which the intuitive perception of knowledge first comes about in the understanding. Foremost of these is the impression of light on the eye, and then colour as a modification of that impression. These then are the affection of the eye, are the effect itself, which exists even without any relation to a cause. The new-born infant has the sensation of light and colour before it intuitively perceives and knows the luminous or coloured object as such. Not even any squinting alters the colour. If the understanding converts the sensation into intuitive perception, then naturally this effect is also related and assigned to its cause, and to the body producing the effect light or colour is attributed as qualities, that is to say, as modes of operation. Yet it is recognized only as that which produces this effect. "The body is red" means that it produces the effect of red colour in the eye. To be is generally synonymous with to act or to operate; therefore even in German everything that *is* is very strikingly and with unconscious profundity described as *actual* (*wirklich*) i.e., as acting. Through our apprehension of colour as something inherent in a body its immediate perception that precedes this is not altered at all; it is and remains an affection of the eye. Merely as the cause of that affection is the object intuitively perceived. But the colour itself is alone the effect, is the state produced in the eye, and as such is independent of the object, which exists only for the understanding; for all intuitive perception is intellectual.

1. Being chapter I of Schopenhauer's essay *Ueber das Sehn und die Farben,* Second Edition, 1854. [Tr.]

2. Cabanis, *Des rapports du physique et du moral: Mémoire,* III, § 5.

3. This concerns the pages Professor Rosas of Vienna appropriated to himself. I have mentioned him and his other plagiarisms in my work *On the Will in Nature* ("Physiology and Pathology").

4. Page 114 of this work. [Tr.]

5. "Spontaneous movement in the taking of food." [Tr.]

SELECTED BIBLIOGRAPHY

I. WORKS OF SCHOPENHAUER

German Editions:

SCHOPENHAUER, Arthur. *Schopenhauers sämtliche Werke*. Edited by Paul Deussen. 13 vols. Munich: R. Piper, 1911-42.

——————— . *Schopenhauers sämtliche Werke*. Edited by Arthur Hübscher. 7 vols. Wiesbaden: F. A. Brockhaus, 1946-50.

——————— . *Schopenhauers handschriftlicher Nachlass*. Edited by Arthur Hübscher. 5 vols. Frankfurt am Main: Waldemar Kramer, 1966--. [Three volumes published to date.]

Translations:

SCHOPENHAUER, Arthur. *Selected Essays of Arthur Schopenhauer*. Translated and edited by E. Belfort. London: Bell & Sons, 1926.

—————————— . *On the Freedom of the Will.* Translated by Konstantin Kolenda. Library of Liberal Arts. New York: Bobbs-Merrill, 1960.

—————————— . *The Pessimist's Handbook: A Collection of Popular Essays.* Translated by T. Bailey Saunders. Edited by Hazel Barnes. Bison Books. Lincoln: University of Nebraska Press, 1964.

—————————— . *On the Basis of Morality.* Translated by E. F. J. Payne. Library of Liberal Arts. New York: Bobbs-Merrill, 1965.

—————————— . *The World as Will and Representation.* Translated by E. F. J. Payne. 2 vols. New York: Dover Publications, 1966.

II. WORKS ON SCHOPENHAUER

BEER, Margrieta. *Schopenhauer.* London: T. C. & E. C. Jack, 1914.

CALDWELL, S. *Schopenhauer's System in its Philosophical Significance.* Edinburgh: F. Blackwood & Sons, 1896.

COPLESTON, Frederick. *Arthur Schopenhauer: Philosopher of Pessimism.* London: Burns, Oates and Washbourne, 1947.

DEUSSEN, Paul. *The Elements of Metaphysics.* London: Macmillan & Co., 1894.

DORING, W. O. *Schopenhauer.* Hamburg: Hansicher Gildenverlag, 1947.

GARDINER, Patrick. *Schopenhauer.* Penguin Books, 1963.

HÜBSCHER, Arthur. *Arthur Schopenhauer: Mensch und Philosoph in seinen Briefen.* Wiesbaden: F. A. Brockhaus, 1960.

───────────. *Schopenhauer: Biographie eines Weltbildes.* Stuttgart: Reclam, 1967.

PFEIFFER, K. *Arthur Schopenhauer: Persönlichkeit und Werk.* Leipzig: A. Kröner, 1925.

SALTUS, Edgar E. *The Philosophy of Disenchantment.* New York: Belford Co., 1885.

SCHMIDT, K. O. *Das Erwachen aus dem Lebens-Traum.* Pfullingen: Baum Verlag, 1957.

TAYLOR, Richard. *The Will to Live.* New York: Anchor Books, 1962.

WAGNER, G. F. *Schopenhauer-Register.* Stuttgart: Fr. Frommann, 1960.

WHITTAKER, Thomas. *Schopenhauer.* London: Constable, 1920.

ZIMMERN, Helen. *Arthur Schopenhauer: His Life and His Philosophy.* London: Longmans, Green & Co., 1876.

ZINT, Hans. *Schopenhauer als Erlebnis.* Munich: E. Reinhardt, 1954.

Index

Index